MW00340481

# Volume the Third

## By Jane Austen

---

*In Her Own Hand*

INTRODUCTION BY
KATHRYN SUTHERLAND

Abbeville Press Publishers
NEW YORK LONDON

EDITOR: Joan Strasbaugh
DESIGN AND TYPESETTING: Ada Rodriguez
PRODUCTION MANAGER: Louise Kurtz

First published in the United States of America in 2014 by Abbeville Press, 137 Varick Street, New York, NY 10013


Printed in Hong Kong.

Extracts taken from *Minor Works*, Jane Austen, collected and edited from the manuscripts by R. W. Chapman (1963) by permission of Oxford University Press.

First edition
10 9 8 7 6 5 4 3 2 1

Library of Congress Cataloging-in-Publication Data

Austen, Jane, 1775–1817.
[Works. Selections]
Volume the third by Jane Austen : in her own hand / Jane Austen ; introduction by Kathryn Sutherland. —First edition.
pages cm —(Jane Austen: in her own hand ; 3)
Summary: "Volume the Third is one of three notebooks written by Jane Austen in her teens. Volume the Third includes 2 stories written in her own hand. An introduction by Kathryn Sutherland and transcription are included"—Provided by publisher.
ISBN 978-0-7892-1201-6 (hardback)
1. Austen, Jane, 1775-1817—Manuscripts—Facsimiles. 2. Manuscripts, English—Facsimiles. I. Title. II. Title: In her own hand.
PR4032 2014c
828'.709—dc23

2014016101

For bulk and premium sales and for text adoption procedures, write to Customer Service Manager, Abbeville Press, 137 Varick Street, New York, NY 10013, or call 1-800-ARTBOOK.

Visit Abbeville Press online at www.abbeville.com.

# CONTENTS

# A NOVELIST OF IDEAS

Jane Austen's *Volume the Third* consists of two early novellas, "Evelyn" and "Kitty, or the Bower," usually referred to by its revised name, "Catharine." Like *Volume the First* and *Volume the Second*, the manuscript takes its name from the inscription on the upper cover of the notebook into which it is written, and at 140 pages it is the shortest of the three. It was also the last of the teenage volumes to be published, as late as 1951.[1] Its two stories—which took shape according to a tight schedule of drafting and copying in 1792, when Austen was sixteen—contain more evidence of immediate composition and look less like fair copies than most of the other teenage pieces. "Evelyn," much the shorter of the two, is abandoned after little more than twenty pages; "Kitty, or the Bower," also unfinished, fills ninety-four pages in Austen's hand. The obvious comparison, in style and dating, is with "The Three Sisters," a piece still in the process of creation as it is set down, entered toward the end of *Volume the First*, perhaps simply because sufficient blank pages remained there to offer it a home.

"Evelyn" is an early experiment in Austen's trademark real estate fiction.[2] Mr. Gower, a gentleman traveler, arriving in a Sussex village where he is completely unknown, in the space of a few lines is pressed to accept food, wine, money, a house and a bride. An absurd tale, its humor lies in its severe abstraction: the characters do not matter; they lack any motive; their exchanges are stripped of all natural relations. But this is thoughtful economy: it is as if the teenage writer is paring back narrative to its bare bones to examine what is essential, and how its elements interact. By contrast, "Kitty, or the Bower" shares with major published novels of the 1790s an imaginative reference to contemporary political debate that makes it a remarkable debut from a sixteen-year-old writer, foreshadowing themes that will emerge in her adult fiction. Versions of three of Austen's novels belong to the 1790s, a decade significant for female intellectual and creative intervention in the ferment of ideas—especially those about education, sexual politics and relations between the sexes—following the French Revolution. Though they would not be published until much later, in the 1810s, *Pride and Prejudice* and *Northanger Abbey* share with "Kitty" a focus on such 1790s issues as the criticism of fashionable accomplishments over proper education for women; the limited prospects for middle-class girls without fortune; and the championship of the novel itself as the legitimate vehicle for the expression of women's views.

---

STEVENTON RECTORY, where Jane Austen composed her juvenilia. An illustration from *A Memoir of Jane Austen* by her nephew James Edward Austen-Leigh, 1871.

The reader is introduced to Kitty Peterson (the name is later revised to Catharine Percival) as she grieves for the loss of one set of friends, Cecilia and Mary Wynne, and eagerly anticipates the arrival of a new companion, Camilla Stanley. The Wynnes were "the daughters of the Clergyman of the Parish" (p. 33)[3]—that is, they occupied a social position similar to that of Jane Austen and her sister Cassandra—while Camilla's parents are "people of Large Fortune & high Fashion" (p. 40). With the departure of the Wynnes, Kitty, described as "a great reader" (p. 42), has lost real friendship and intelligent discussion. Camilla, by contrast, is a vapid socialite whose talk is all of shopping and holidays, balls and dresses and her glittering social connections. The eldest Miss Wynne has been shipped out to India to find a husband among the British officials working there, while her sister has become a lady's companion—little better than a servant—to the daughters of a rich relation. We never meet the Wynnes, but their fate forms a topic of discussion between Kitty and Camilla and serves to emphasize the polemical role Austen's latest heroine fills. Here she remonstrates with Camilla, who has mindlessly dismissed the Wynne girls as "the luckiest Creatures in the World":

> "But do you call it lucky, for a Girl of Genius & Feeling to be sent in quest of a Husband to Bengal, to be married there to a Man of whose Disposition she has no opportunity of judging till her Judgement is of no use to her, who may be a Tyrant, or a Fool or both for what she knows to the Contrary. Do you call that fortunate?" (p. 54)

The question came very near to home for the young Jane Austen, whose own aunt had been sent to India on similar terms in 1752. Through Kitty she makes it clear that there is nothing to be grateful for in the terms upon which the Wynnes have secured their future: one is sent abroad to marry the first man who will take her, while her sister is "Dependant even for her Cloathes on the bounty of others" (p. 56).

Decades later, the mature novelist confronts the same stark truth: that economic security—money—must be women's first concern. Austen never suggests that the world is well lost for love. This message complicates any simple reading of romantic love in *Pride and Prejudice*. We may laugh at Mrs. Bennet's foolish husband-hunting, but what choice has she got, when Mr. Bennet has been so negligent in providing for their daughters? Charlotte Lucas accepts objectionable Mr. Collins because marriage, "however uncertain of giving happiness," must be her "pleasantest preservative from want." At the same time, her brothers rejoice because they are "relieved from their apprehension of Charlotte's dying an old maid"—by which we are to understand that they are "relieved" from the burden of her maintenance themselves (*Pride and Prejudice*, chapter 22). After the freakish comedy of the earlier juvenilia, where active, unchaste heroines, by force of energy and will, turn their little worlds upside down, we sense in "Kitty, or the Bower" a satire more reflective of things as they are and, in consequence, more effective.

In "Kitty," Austen begins to examine the stifling limitations imposed by women's dependency—a subject that will last her a lifetime.

"Kitty," in fact, shares subject and emphasis with "Letter the third From A young Lady in distress'd Circumstances to her freind," one of "A Collection of Letters" in *Volume the Second* (pp. 202–11). Experiments in character study, these letters each test a mood or state of mind; the substance of this particular letter is the unsparing attempts of Lady Greville to bully and humiliate Maria Williams (the letter writer), making public her poverty and inferior social status. This is a topic Austen will return to in Lady Catherine de Bourgh's intimidation of Charlotte Lucas and Elizabeth Bennet in *Pride and Prejudice*. Like the mature writer, the young Austen was an adept recycler of phrase, motif and incident. A more immediate redeployment of this theme lies in the character of Kitty Peterson and her relations to the Stanleys, especially to Camilla Stanley, who is privileged and wellborn, while Kitty (like Maria Williams) is merely the daughter of a merchant.

But what is so unusual about "Kitty, or the Bower" in Austen's work as a whole is how its oppressive domestic politics and its keen sense of the inadequacies of women's education and opportunities, as exemplified in different ways by the situations of the Wynne girls, Kitty and Camilla, are contextualized within a broader, highly topical national politics. Kitty's aunt's exaggerated anti-Jacobin views and fears of imminent social and moral collapse echo those of many conservative writers of the time who, like her, called for a renewal of national standards at the personal level. These views, a direct rejection of calls for radical reform inspired by the French Revolution of 1789, act as a refrain to every slight liberty she suspects Kitty of taking:

> "every thing is going to sixes & sevens and all order will soon be at an end throughout the Kingdom."
>
> "Not however Ma'am the sooner, I hope, from any conduct of mine, said Catherine in a tone of great humility, for upon my honour I have done nothing this evening that can contribute to overthrow the establishment of the kingdom."
>
> "You are mistaken Child, replied she; the welfare of every Nation depends upon the virtue of it's individuals, and any one who offends in so gross a manner against decorum & propriety, is certainly hastening it's ruin. You have been giving a bad example to the World, and the World is but too well disposed to receive such." (p. 110)

The subject is couched as a joke, but it does not disguise the fact that in "Kitty, or the Bower" we discover the young Jane Austen responding with unexpected openness to the political climate of 1792, when the debate over social rights, and criticism of their repression, was at its height.[4]

---

All three notebooks are sociable performances, their contents designed to be shared. In extravagant dedications, Jane Austen spins fanciful and provocative connections to an immediate community of readers—family and friends, many of them living in or near her first home in Steventon, Hampshire—whom she imagines as sponsors of her writings. Only *Volume the Third* suggests a different kind of joint enterprise, whereby the creative and editorial interventions of a new generation transformed this notebook into a shared writing space.[5] The real challenge it offers the reader is to separate renewed authorial interest in the manuscript across a distance in time from the intrusions of others—and, specifically, to distinguish the different hands at work.

Critics have long recognized substantial continuations to both stories, inserted years after their initial composition, in the hands of Anna Austen (later Anna Lefroy) and her younger half brother James Edward Austen (later James Edward Austen-Leigh). But it now seems probable that many small local revisions to the manuscript—including such important details as the change of title from "Kitty, or the Bower" to "Catharine, or the Bower," and the renaming of Kitty Peterson as Catharine Percival—assumed by previous editors to be Austen's own, were also introduced by another hand, most likely James Edward's.[6]

As the children of her eldest brother James Austen, Anna and James Edward grew up close to Aunt Jane. In 1801 they moved into the Steventon parsonage when their father took over clerical duties there, his father, George Austen, having retired with his wife and daughters to Bath. Even earlier, after the death of her mother when she was only two, Anna (her aunt's namesake, christened Jane Anna Elizabeth Austen) had come to live at Steventon with aunts Jane and Cassandra; earlier still, at just six weeks of age, she became the unwitting dedicatee of two miniature mock-didactic stories, "Miscellanious [sic] Morsels," in *Volume the First*. There is ample evidence that Anna was Aunt Jane's willing pupil throughout her childhood and teenage years, and that habits of shared oral and written composition began early between them. They collaborated on the playlet "Sir Charles Grandison," written after 1800, when Anna was only seven years old. Anna's unfinished continuation to "Evelyn" is written onto four leaves of varying sizes loosely inserted at the end of *Volume the Third* and signed with the initials "*J A E L*" (Jane Anna Elizabeth Lefroy), indicating a date after her marriage in November 1814, at the age of twenty-one, to Ben Lefroy.[7] Long after Austen's death, Anna would attempt a continuation of her aunt's final manuscript, *Sanditon*.[8]

The teenage James Edward also tried his hand at short stories and novels, portions of which survive, occasionally sending them for comment and approval to Aunt Jane.[9] After breaking off "Evelyn" at page 21, Austen left the next nine pages blank, beginning "Catharine" at [page 30].[10] At some later date, seven of these blanks were filled (pp. 21–[27]), completing "Evelyn" in a competent pastiche of Austen's comic style. The hand is now agreed to be James Edward Austen's; so too is that of the final four pages of the unfinished ending to "Kitty, or the Bower" and its revision as "Catharine" (pp. 124–27).

These revisions and additions would have been made after Austen went to live in Chawton in July 1809; many can be dated, either by internal reference or by hand. For example, two alterations in "Kitty"—Camilla Stanley's reference to a "new Regency walking dress" (replacing an original reference to a "Pierrot" on page 67, a reading only recently deciphered by Jenny McAuley)[11] and the deletion of an allusion to "Seccar's explanation of the Catechism" (Thomas Secker's *Lectures on the Catechism of the Church of England*, 1769) and substitution of "Coelebs in Search of a Wife" (p. 109)—were only possible, respectively, after February 5, 1811, the date of the Regency Act, and after the December 1808 publication of Hannah More's *Coelebs in Search of a Wife*.

In 1811 Jane Austen became a published author with *Sense and Sensibility*. By 1816 she had four novels before the public, and a growing reputation as a serious writer. But habits of family composition persisted in occasional verses and in the comic "Plan of a Novel," probably written in early 1816, soon after the publication of *Emma*. Such home-directed pieces imply a circle of family and friends reading, laughing over and commenting on the author's performance, just as they did twenty-five years before. In allowing her niece and nephew, Anna and James Edward, to try their hands at continuing the stories in *Volume the Third*, and even permitting James Edward to edit "Kitty, or the Bower," Jane Austen confirmed for the next generation of scribbling Austens the original function of her notebooks: to nurture authorship within family life. At the same time she was developing in print a different, independent authority. Jane Austen's teenage writings remained treasured family possessions, in some cases until late in the twentieth century. Facsimile publication extends the lives of these three notebooks to all her readers, allowing them to trace her hand across the page, to examine her corrections and revisions and to enjoy in all its aspects her playful apprenticeship in the art of bookmaking.

This facsimile edition of *Volume the Third* has been produced with care to match the size of the original notebook, the appearance of its paper and the brown-black color of the iron gall ink that Jane Austen used. The transcription following the manuscript is that of the great twentieth-century Austen scholar Robert W. Chapman. Chapman was the first to edit Jane Austen's manuscripts in full and his early editions now have classic status.

NOTES

1. The manuscript's contents were briefly described and the dedication and first paragraph of "Kitty, or the Bower" first printed in the Austen family biography, William Austen-Leigh and Richard Arthur Austen-Leigh's *Jane Austen: Her Life and Letters; A Family Record* (London: Smith, Elder, 1913), pp. 55–57. But *Volume the Third* was only published in 1951, by R. W. Chapman, in an edition uniform with his earlier transcriptions of the mature fiction manuscripts and *Volume the First*. The notebook itself remained in Austen family hands until 1976. It is now held in the British Library, London, Add. MS. 65381. For information on its physical appearance, history and ownership, see the head note to *Volume the Third*, available at www.janeausten.ac.uk, the Digital Edition of Jane Austen's Fiction Manuscripts, ed. Kathryn Sutherland (2010).

2. Marjorie Garber uses the phrase "real estate literature" in "The Jane Austen Syndrome," in *Quotation Marks* (New York: Routledge, 2003), pp. 199–200.

3. Parenthentical page numbers refer to Jane Austen's own pagination of the notebook.

4. "The twelve-month period beginning in February 1792 was the *annus mirabilis* of eighteenth-century radicalism, for it saw not only the appearance of its classic texts, but the peak activity of radical associations, in London and in the provinces, which were now for the first time not merely joined but run by working men." Marilyn Butler, *Burke, Paine, Godwin, and the Revolution Controversy* (Cambridge, England: Cambridge University Press, 1984), p. 7.

5. Margaret Anne Doody originally made the suggestion that, in the company of the next generation, these notebooks may have been transformed into "something a little like a very informal writing class." Doody and Douglas Murray, ed., *Catharine and Other Writings* (Oxford, England: Oxford University Press, 1993), p. xx.

6. See Kathryn Sutherland, "From Kitty to Catharine: James Edward Austen's Hand in *Volume the Third*," *Review of English Studies*, available online from September 2014.

7. Anna Lefroy's four leaves are digitized and transcribed at http://www.janeausten.ac.uk/manuscripts/blvolthird/21a.html.

8. For Anna Austen's collaborations with her aunt, see Kathryn Sutherland, *Jane Austen's Textual Lives: From Aeschylus to Bollywood* (Oxford, England: Oxford University Press, 2005), pp. 224–25, 246–48.

9. *Jane Austen's Letters*, ed. Deirdre Le Faye, 3rd ed. (Oxford, England: Oxford University Press, 1995), pp. 323, 325. Portions survive from several of James Edward Austen's teenage manuscript fictions in Winchester, Hampshire Record Office, 23M93/86/6/1–5. Some are dateable by hand and by paper to 1812–17, when he was aged thirteen to eighteen.

10. Square brackets are used to indicate inferred pagination where the normal continuous manuscript pagination is absent.

11. Jenny McAuley, " 'A Long Letter upon a Jacket and a Petticoat': Reading Beneath Some Deletions in the Manuscript of 'Catharine, or The Bower,' " *Persuasions: The Jane Austen Journal* 31 (2009): pp. 191–98.

Volume the Third

II

Effusions of Fancy

By a very Young Lady

Consisting of Tales

in a Style entirely new

for James Edward Austen

Jane Austen – May 6th 1792.

1

Contents

To Miss Mary Lloyd,

The following Novel is by permission

Dedicated,

by her Obed.t humble Serv.t

The Author

# Evelyn

In a retired part of the County of Sussex
there is a village (for what I know to the
ntrary) called Evelyn, perhaps one of the most
eautiful spots in the south of England. A
entleman passing through it on horseback
bout twenty years ago, was so entirely of my
inion in this respect, that he put up at the
ittle Alehouse in it & enquired with great ear
estness whether there were any house to be
tt in the Parish. The Landlady, who as well
s every one else in Evelyn was remarkably
miable, shook her head at this question, but
eemed unwilling to give him any answer.
e could not bear this uncertainty - yet knew
t how to obtain the information he desired.
repeat a question which had already appear

to make the good woman uneasy was im
:possible—. He turned from her in visible a
:gitation. "What a situation am I in!" sa
he to himself as he walked to the windo
and threw up the sash. He found himse
vived by the Air, which he felt to a mu
greater degree when he had opened the win
:dow than he had done before. Yet it wa
but for a moment—. The agonizing ~~[illegible]~~ pain of
Doubt & Suspence again weighed down his
Spirits. The good woman who had watche
in eager silence every turn of his Countena
with that benevolence which characterize
the inhabitants of Evelyn, intreated him t
tell her the cause of his uneasiness. "Is
there anything Sir in my power to do th
may relieve your Greifs—Tell me in wha
manner I can sooth them, & believe me th
the friendly balm of Comfort and Assistance sh

t be wanting; for indeed Sir I have a impathetic Soul."

Amiable Woman (said Mr Gower, affected lmost to tears by this generous offer) his Greatness of mind in one to whom I n almost a Stranger, serves but to make e the more warmly wish for a house in his sweet village — What would I not give be your Neighbour, to be blessed with your cquaintance, and with the farther know: ledge of your Virtues! Oh! with what pleasure ould I form myself by such an example! ll me then, best of Women, is there no ossibility? — — I cannot speak — You know y Meaning —."

Alas! Sir, replied Mrs Willis, there is none. ery house in this village, from the sweetness f the Situation, & the purity of the Air, in hich neither Misery, Ill health, or Vice are er wafted, is inhabited. And yet, (after a shor

pause) there is a Family, who tho' warmly attached to the spot, yet from a peculi-
Generosity of Disposition would perhaps be
willing to oblige You with ~~the reversion~~ their house.
~~of their house~~." He eagerly caught at the
idea, and having gained a direction to the
~~them~~ place, he set off immediately on his walk
to it. As he approached the House, he was
delighted with its situation. It was in the
exact center of a small circular paddock
which was enclosed by a regular paling, &
bordered with a plantation of Lombardy poplars, & Spruce firs alternately placed in thr
rows. A gravel walk ran through this
beautiful Shrubbery, and as the remainder of the paddock was unincumbered
with any other Timber, the surface of it
perfectly even & smooth, and grazed by four
white Cows which were disposed at equal
distances from each other, the whole appear

nce, of the place as Mr Gower entered the
ddock was uncommonly striking. A beau
ifully-rounded, gravel road without any
n or interruption led immediately to the
use. Mr Gower rang—the Door was soon
ened. "Are Mr & Mrs Webb at home?"
ry Good Sir they are" replied the Servant;
nd leading the way, conducted Mr Gower
 stairs into a very elegant Dressing room,
here a Lady rising from her seat, welcomed
im with all the Generosity which Mrs
illis had attributed to the Family.
Welcome best of Men—Welcome to this
ouse, & to every thing it contains. William
ll your Master of the happiness I enjoy—
invite him to partake of it—Bring up some
ocolate immediately; Spread a Cloth in the dining
rlour, and carry in the venison pasty—In the mean
ime let the Gentleman have some sandwiches, and
ring in a Basket of Fruit—Send up some Ices and

a bason of Soup, and do not forget some Jellies a
Cakes." Then turning to Mr Gower, & taking out a
purse, "Accept this my good Sir, — Believe me you
are welcome to everything that is in my pow
to bestow. — I wish my purse were weightier, but
Mr Webb must make up my deficiences. — I know
he has cash in the house to the amount of an h
:dred pounds, which he shall bring you immedi
:ately." Mr Gower felt overpowered by her generosit
as he put the purse in his pocket, and from the
:~~fu~~ excess of his Gratitude, could scarcely express him
intelligibly when he accepted her offer of a the hun
:dred pounds. Mr Webb soon entered the room, an
repeated every protestation of Freindship & Cordiality
which his Lady had ~~before expressed~~ already made. — The Chocolate
The Sandwiches, the Jellies, the Cakes, the Ice, and
Soup soon made their appearance, and Mr Gower
having tasted something of all, and pocketted the
rest, was conducted into the dining parlour, wh
he eat a most excellent Dinner & partook of the
most exquisite Wines, while Mr and Mrs Webb

tood by him still pressing him to eat and rink a little more. "And now my good Sir, said r Webb, when Mr Gower's repast was concluded, hat else can we do to contribute to your happi: ess and express the Affection we bear for you. ll us what you wish more to receive, and depend on our gratitude for the communication of your ishes." "Give me then your house & Grounds; sk for nothing else." "It is yours, exclaimed th at once; from this moment it is yours." This reement concluded on and the present accepted by r Gower, Mr Webb rang to have the Carriage dered, telling William at the same time to ll the Young Ladies.

Best of Men, said Mrs Webb, we will not long itrude upon your Time."

Make no Apologies dear Madam, replied Mr ower, You are welcome to stay this half hour l you like it."

They both burst forth into raptures of Admiration

at his politeness, which they agreed served o
to make their Conduct appear more inexc
:sable in trespassing on his time.

The Young Ladies soon entered the room.
The eldest of them was about seventeen, t
other, several years younger. Mr Gower had
no sooner fixed his Eyes on Miss Webb than
felt that something more was necess
to his happiness than the house he ha
just received. Mrs Webb introduced hi
to her daughter. "Our dear freind Mr Gow
my Love — He has been so good as to a
:cept of this house, small as it is
to promise to "keep it for ever" "Give me leave to a
:sure you Sir, said Miss Webb, that I am
highly sensible of your kindness in th
respect, which from the shortness of m
Father's & Mother's acquaintance with
you, is more than usually flattering.

r Gower bowed — "You are too obliging
a'am — I assure you that I like the house
xtremely — and if they would complete
heir generosity by giving me their eldest
ughter in marriage with a handsome
rtion, I should have nothing more to
ish for." This compliment brought a
lush into the cheeks of the lovely Miss
ebb, who seemed however to refer herself
her father & Mother. They looked delighted
t each other — At length Mrs Webb breaking
lence, said — "We bend under a weight
f obligations to you which we can never
pay. Take our girl, take our Maria, and
n her must the difficult task fall, of
ndeavouring to make some return to so
uch Beneficence." Mr Webb added, "Her
tune is but ten thousand pounds, which
s almost too small a sum to be offered."

This objection however being instantly
:moved by the generosity of Mr Gower, wh
declared himself satisfied with the sum
:tioned, Mr & Mrs Webb, with their young
daughter took their leave, and on the ne
day, the nuptials of their eldest with M
Gower were celebrated. — This amiable Man
now found himself perfectly happy; united to a
very lovely and deserving young woman, with a
handsome fortune, an elegant house, settled in the
village of Evelyn, & by that means enabled to
cultivate his acquaintance with Mrs Willis, cou
he have a wish ungratified? — For some month
he found that he could not, till one day as he
was walking in the Shrubbery with Maria lea
:ing on his arm, they observed a rose full-bl
lying on the gravel; it had fallen from a rose tr
which with three others had been planted by
Mr Webb to give a pleasing variety to the
walk. These four Rose trees served also to mark
the quarters of the Shrubbery, by which mean

the Traveller might always know how far in
is progress round the Paddock he was got -.
Maria stooped to pick up the beautifull flower,
nd with all her Family Generosity presented it
 her Husband. "My dear Frederic, said she, pray
ke this charming rose." "Rose! exclaimed the
wer -. Oh! Maria, of what does not that remind
! alas my poor Sister, how have I neglected
m!" The truth was that Mr Gower was the
ly son of a very large Family, of which Miss
ose Gower was the thirteenth daughter. This
oung Lady whose merits deserved a better fate
han she met with, was the darling of her re:
lations - From the clearness of her skin & the
rilliancy of her Eyes, she was fully entitled
 all their partial affection. Another circum:
tance contributed to the general Love they bore
r, and that was one of the finest heads of hair
 the world. A few Months before her Brother's
arriage, her heart had been engaged by the at:
tentions and charms of a young Man whose high

rank and expectations seemed to foretell ob
:jections from his Family to a match which
would be highly desirable to theirs. Proposa
were made on the young Man's part, and pr
:per objections on his Father's - He was desired
to return from Carlisle where he was with
his beloved Rose, to the family seat in Suss
He was obliged to comply, and the angry F
:ther then finding from his Conversation ho
determined he was to marry no other woma
sent him for a fortnight to the Isle of Wight
under the care of the Family Chaplain, wi
the hope of overcoming his Constancy by Ti
and Absence in a foreign Country. They accord
:ingly prepared to bid a long adieu to Englan
The young Nobleman was not allowed to see
his Rosa. They set sail — A storm arose
which baffled the arts of the Seamen. The
Vessel was wrecked on the coast of Calsho
and every Soul on board perished. This sad
Event soon reached Carlisle, and the beautif

Rose was affected by it, beyond the power of pression. It was to soften her affliction by ob: taining a picture of her unfortunate Lover hat her brother undertook a Journey into ussex, where he hoped that his petition ould not be rejected, by the severe yet afflict: d Father. When he reached Evelyn he as not many miles from —— Castle, but he pleasing events which befell him in hat place had for a while made him totally rget the object of his Journey & his unhappy ister. The little incident of the rose however rought everything concerning her to his recol: lection again, & he bitterly repented his neg: lect. He returned to the house immediately nd agitated ~~with~~ by Greif, Apprehension and Shame rote the following Letter to Rosa.

July 14th — Evelyn

My dearest Sister

As it is now four months since left Carlisle, during which period I have not once written to you. You will perhaps un:justly accuse me of Neglect and Forgetfulness. Alas! I blush when I own the truth of your accusation. — Yet if you are still alive, do not think too harshly of me, or suppose that I could for a moment forget the situation of my Rose. Believe me I will forget you no longer, but ~~will~~ hasten as soon as possible to — Castle if I find by your answer that you are still alive. Maria joins me in every dutiful and affectionate wish, & I am yours sincerely

F. Gower.

He waited in the most anxious expecta:tion for an answer to his Letter, which arrived as soon as the great distance from Carlisle would admit of. — But alas, it came not ~~for~~ from Rosa.

Carlisle July 17th

Dear Brother

My Mother has taken the liberty of opening your Letter to poor Rose, as she has b

dead these six weeks. Your long absence and
ntinued Silence gave us all great uneasiness
d hastened her to the Grave. Your Journey
— Castle therefore may be spared. You do
t tell us where you have been since the
ime of your quitting Carlisle, nor in any
way account for your tedious absence, which
ives us some Surprise. We all unite in
Compts to Maria, & beg to know who she is —.

Yr affec:te Sister

M. Gower.

This Letter, by which Mr Gower was obliged to
ttribute to his own conduct, his Sisters death,
as so violent a shock to his feelings, that in
pite of his living at Evelyn where Illness was
arcely ever heard of, he was attacked by a fit
 the Gout, which confining him to his own
om afforded an opportunity to Maria of shining
 that favourite character of Sir Charles Gran:
sons, a nurse. No woman could ever appear
ore amiable than Maria did under such
ircumstances, and at last by her unremitting

attentions had the pleasure of seeing him gr
:dually recover the use of his feet. It was a
blessing by no means lost on him, for he wa
no sooner in a condition to leave the house,
than he mounted his horse, and rode to —— Ca
:tle, wishing to find whether his Lordship
softened by his Son's death, might have been
brought to consent to the match, had both
and Rosa been alive. His amiable Maria
followed him with her Eyes tile she could
him no longer, and then sinking into her
chair overwhelmed with Greif, found that in
absence she could enjoy no comfort.

Mr Gower arrived late in the even
at the castle, which was situated on a woo
Eminence commanding a beautiful prospec
of the Sea. Mr Gower did not dislike the
situation, tho' it was certainly greatly ~~su~~
:~~perior~~ inferior to that of his own house. There w
an irregularity in the fall of the ground

nd a profusion of old Timber which appeared
him illsuited to the stile of the Castle, for
being a building of a very ~~old~~ ancient date, he
ought it required the Paddock of Evelyn lodge
form a Contrast, and enliven the structure.
he gloomy appearance of the old Castle frown:
ing on him as he followed it's winding ap:
roach, struck him with terror. Nor did he
ink himself safe, tile he was introduced
ito ~~the~~ Drawing room where the Family
ere assembled to tea. Mr Gower was a
erfect Stranger to every one in the Circle
t tho' he was always timid in the Dark
d easily terrified when alone, he did not
nt that more necessary & more noble Cour:
ge which enabled him without a Blush
enter a large party of superior Rank, whom
had never seen before, & to take his Seat
mongst them with perfect Indifference.
he name of Gower was not unknown to
nd — . He felt distressed & astonished; yet

rose and received him with all the politeness
of a well-bred Man. Lady — who felt a deeper
sorrow at the loss of her Son, than his Lord
harder heart was capable of, could hardly ke
her Seat when she found that he was the
Brother of her lamented ~~[illegible]~~ Henry's Rosa. "My Lo
said Mr Gower as soon as he was seated, Y
are perhaps surprised at receiving a visit
from a Man whom you could not have t
least expectation of seeing here. But my Sis
my unfortunate Sister is the real cause of
my thus troubling you: That luckless Gi
is now no more - and tho' She can receiv
no pleasure from the intelligence, yet for t
Satisfaction of her Family I wish to know
whether the Death of this unhappy Pair
has made an impression on your heart suf
:iciently strong to obtain that consent to
their Marriage which in happier circum
:stances you would not be persuaded to g

pposing that they now were both alive":
is Lordship seemed lossed in astonishment.
dy — could not support the mention of
r son, and left the room in tears; the
t of the Family remained attentively
tening, almost persuaded that Mr Gower
s distracted. "Mr Gower, replied his Lordship
his is a very odd question — It appears to
e that you are supposing an impossibility —
o one can more sincerely regret the death
f my Son than I have always done, and
gives me great concern to know that
iss Gower's was hastened by his — . Yet to
ppose them alive is destroying at once the
otive for a change in my sentiments con:
rning the affair." "My Lord, replied Mr
wer in anger, I see that you are a most
flexible Man, and that not even the death
f your Son can make you wish his future
ife happy. I will no longer detain your Lord=
=ship

I see, I plainly see that you are a very vile
Man – And now I have the honour of wishin
all your Lordships, and Ladyships a good Nigh
He immediately left the room, forgetting in
heat of his Anger the lateness of the hou
which at any other time would have ma
him tremble, & leaving the whole Company
unanimous in their opinion of his being
When however he had mounted his horse
and the great Gates of the Castle had shut
him out, he felt an universal tremor thr
out his whole frame. If we consider his
Situation indeed, alone, on horseback, as la
in the year as August, and in the day, as n
o'clock, with no light to direct him bu
that of the Moon almost full, and the s
which alarmed him by their twinkling, w
can refrain from pitying him? – No hous
within a quarter of a mile, and a Gloom
Castle blackened by the deep shade of Waln

nd Pines, behind him. — He felt indeed al:
most distracted with his fears, and shutting
s Eyes till he arrived at the Village to pre:
ent his seeing either Gipsies or Ghosts, he
de on a full gallop all the way. On his stet
turn home, he rang the housebell, but
one appeared, a second time he rang, but
e door was not opened, a third & a fourth
th as little success, when observing the dining
rlour window open he leapt in, &
rsued his way through the house till
reached Maria's Dressingroom, where
found all the servants assembled at tea
rprized at so very unusual a sight, he
inted, on his recovery he found himself
the Sofa, with his wife's maid kneeling
him, chafing his temples with Hungary
ater ——— From her he learned that
s beloved Maria had been so much grieved
his departure that she died of a broken
art about 3 hours after his departure

He then became sufficiently composed
to give necessary orders for her funeral
which took place the Monday following
this being the Saturday - When Mr Youle
had settled the order of the procession
he set out himself to Carlisle, to give
vent to his sorrow in the bosom of his
family - He arrived there in high hea
& spirits, after a delightful journey of
days &c - What was his surprize
on entering the Breakfast parlour to
see Rosa his beloved Rosa seated on a
~~[illegible]~~ Sofa; at the sight of him
she fainted & would have fallen had
not a Gentleman sitting with his back
to the door, started up & saved her from
sinking to the ground - She very soon
came to herself & then introduced this
gentleman to her Brother as her
Husband a Mr Davenport -

But my dearest Rosa said the astonished
over, I thought you were dead & buried.
Why my dr Frederick replied Rosa I wished
ou to think so, hoping that you would
read the report about the country &
 would thus by some means reach
 Castle — By this I hoped some how
 other to touch the hearts of its inhabitants
 was not till the day before yesterday
hat I heard of the death of my beloved
enry which I learned from Mr D—
ho concluded by offering me his hand
ccepted it with transport, & was
arried yesterday —— Mr Gower embraced
is sister & shook hands with Mr Davenport
then took a stroll into the town — As he
assed by a public house he called for
pot of beer, which was brought him
mediately by his old friend Mr Willis —
reat was his astonishment at seeing

Mrs Willis in Carlisle — But not forgetful of the respect he owed her, he dropped on one knee, & received the frothy cup from her, more grateful to him than Nectar — He instantly made her an offer of his hand & heart, which she graciously condescended to accept, telling him that she was only on a visit to her cousin, who kept the Anchor & should be ready to return to Evelyn, whenever he chose — The next morning they were married & immediately proceeded to Evelyn — When he reached home, he recollected that he had never written to Mr & Mrs Webb to inform them of the death of their daughter, which he rightly supposed they knew nothing of, as they never took in any newspaper. He immediately dispatched the following Letter —

Evelyn – Augst 19th 1809–

Dearest Madam,

How can words express
the poignancy of my feelings! Our
aria, our beloved Maria is no
ore, she breathed her last, on Saturday
e 12th of Augst— I see you now in an
gony of grief lamenting not your
wn, but my loss— Rest satisfied
m happy, possessed of my lovely Sarah
hat more can I wish for—

I remain

respectfully Yours

F. Gower

Westgate Build[gs] Aug[st] 22 –

Generous, best of Men

how truly we rejoice to hear of your present welfare & happiness. & how truly grateful are we for your unexampled generosity in writing to condole with us on the late unlucky accident which befel our Maria – I have enclosed a draught on our banker for 30 pounds, which Mr Webb joins with me in entreating you & the amiable Sarah to accept ——

Your most grateful

Anne Augusta Webb

Mr & Mrs Gower resided many years
t Evelyn enjoying perfect happiness the just reward of their virtues
The only alteration which took place
t Evelyn was that Mr & Mrs Davin-
port settled there in Mrs Willis's
former abode & were for many
ears the proprietors of the
White house Inn ——

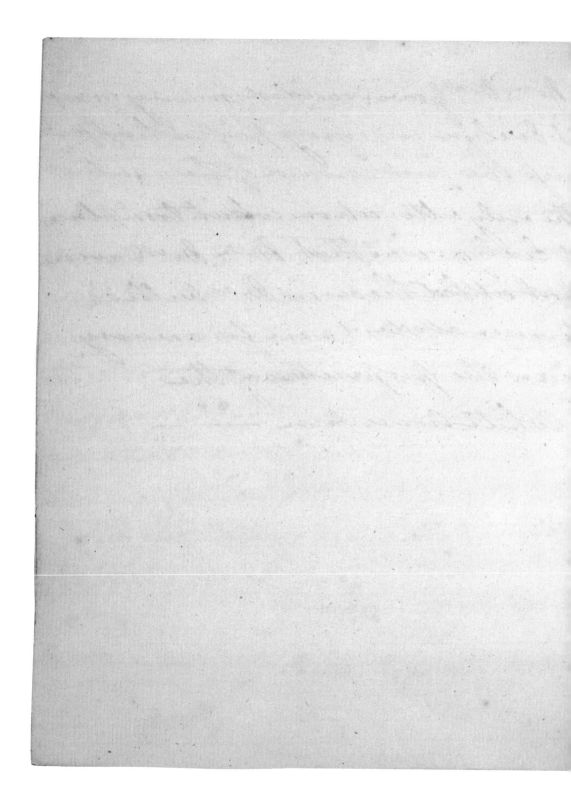

To Miss Austen

Madam

Encouraged by your warm patronag
of The beautiful Cassandra, and The History
England, which through your generous sup
:port, have obtained a place in every li
:brary in the Kingdom, and run through
threescore Editions, I take the liberty of beg
:ging the same Exertions in favour of th
following Novel, which I humbly flatter
myself, possesses Merit beyond any alrea
published, or any that will ever in futur
appear, except such as may proceed from
pen of Your most Grateful Humble Serv

The Autho

Steventon August 1792 —

# Catharine
# ~~Kitty~~, or the Bower

~~Kitty~~ Catharine had the misfortune, as many heroines ve had before her, of losing her Parents when she s very young, and of being brought up under the re of a Maiden Aunt, who while she tenderly ved her, watched over her conduct with so scru: nizing a severity, as to make it very doubtful many people, and to ~~Kitty~~ Catharine amongst the rest, hether she loved her or not. She had frequently en deprived of a real pleasure through this jealous ution, had been sometimes obliged to relinquish Ball because an Officer was to be there, or to ance with a Partner of her Aunt's introduction preference to one of her own Choice. But her pirits were naturally good, and not easily de: ressed, and she possessed such a fund of vivacity nd good humour as could only be damped by me very serious vexation. — Besides these antidotes against every disappointment, and con:solations under them, she had another, which af:forded her constant relief in all her misfortunes and that was a fine shady Bower, the work of her own infantine Labours assisted by those of two young Companions who had resided in the same village—. To this ~~Garden~~ Bower, which termin:ed a very pleasant and retired walk in her Aunt's Garden, she always wandered whenever anything disturbed her, and it possessed such a charm over her senses, as constantly to tranquillize her mind & quiet her spirits— Solitude & reflection might perhaps have had the same effect in her Bed Chamber, yet Habit had so strengthened the idea which Fancy had first suggested, that such a thought never oc:curred to Kitty who was firmly persuaded that her Bower alone could restore her to herself. Her imagination was warm, and in her Friend:ships, as well as in the whole tenure of her Mind, she was enthousiastic. This beloved Bower had been the united work of herself

amiable Girls, for whom since her earliest
ars, she had felt the tenderest regard. They
e the daughters of the Clergyman of the Parish
th whose Family, while it had continued there,
Aunt had been on the most intimate terms,
d the little Girls tho' separated for the greatest
t of the Year by the different Modes of their
cation, were constantly together during the
Days of the Miss Wynnes; ~~they were compa:~~
~~ions in their walks, their Schemes and Amuse:~~
~~ents, and while the sweetness of their disposi:~~
~~ions had prevented any serious Quarrels, the trifling~~
~~isputes which it was impossible wholly to avoid,~~
~~d been far from lessening their affection.~~ In those
ays of happy Childhood, now so often regretted by Kitty
is arbour had been formed, and separated perhaps
ever from these dear freinds, it encouraged more
an any other place the tender and Melancholy
collections of hours rendered pleasant by them, at
e so sorrowful, yet so soothing! It was now two
ars since the death of Mr Wynne, and the conse
uent dispersion of his Family who had been left by

it in great distress. They had been reduced to a st
of absolute dependance on some relations, who thou
very opulent, and very nearly connected with them
had with difficulty been prevailed on to contrib
anything towards their support. Mrs Wynne w
fortunately spared the knowledge & participation
of their distress, by her release from a painful
illness a few months before the death of her hu
:band. — The eldest daughter had been oblig
to accept the offer of one of her cousins to equip
her for the East Indies, and tho' infinitely again
her inclinations had been necessitated to embrac
the only possibility that was offered to her,
a Maintenance; Yet it was one, so opposite
to all her ideas of Propriety, so contrary to he
Wishes, so repugnant to her feelings, that she
would almost have preferred Servitude to it, ha
Choice been allowed her —. Her personal attract
had gained her a husband as soon as she had a
:rived at Bengal, and she had now been marrie
nearly a twelvemonth. Splendidly, yet unhapp
married. United to a Man of double her own a
whose disposition was not amiable, and whose

nners were unpleasing. though his Character
s respectable. Kitty had heard twice from her
nd since her marriage, but her Letters were al:
ays unsatisfactory, and though she did not openly
ss her feelings, yet every line proved her to be
happy. She spoke with pleasure of nothing,
of those Amusements which they had shared
ther and which could return no more, and seemd
have no happiness in view but that of returning
England again. Her sister had been taken by
ther relation the Dowager Lady Halifax as a Com:
nion to her Daughters, and had accompanied
family into Scotland about the same time of
ilia's leaving England. From Mary therefore Kitty
d the power of hearing more frequently, but her
tters were scarcely more comfortable—. There was
t indeed that hopelessness of sorrow in her situation
in her sisters; she was not married, and could
t look forward to a change in her circumstances,
t situated for the present without any immediate
e of it, in a family where, tho' all were her
ations she had no friend, she wrote usually in
pressed Spirits, which her separation from her Sister

and her Sister's Marriage had greatly contribute[d]
to make so. — Divided thus from the two she lo[ved]
best on Earth, while Cecilia & Mary were still m[ore]
endeared to her by their loss, every thing that b[ore]
a remembrance of them was doubly cherished, [&]
the Shrubs they had planted, & the keepsakes th[ey]
had given were rendered sacred —. The living [of]
Chetwynde was now in the possession of a M[r]
Dudley, whose Family unlike the Wynnes we[re]
productive only of vexation & trouble to Mrs Percival
and her Neice. Mr Dudley, who was the youn[ger]
Son of a very noble Family, of a Family m[ore]
famed for their Pride than their opulence, ten[a]-
:cious of his Dignity, and jealous of his rights, w[as]
forever quarrelling, if not with Mrs P. he[re]
with her Steward and Tenants concerning tyth[es]
and with the principal Neighbours themse[lves]
concerning the respect & parade, he exacted.
His Wife, an ill-educated, untaught woma[n]
of ancient family, was proud of that famil[y]
almost without knowing why, and like hi[m]
too was haughty and quarrelsome, without

dering for what. Their only daughter, who in:
ited the ignorance, the insolence, & pride of
ents, was from that Beauty of which she was
easonably vain, considered by them as an
sistable Creature, and looked up to as the fu:
e restorer, by a Splendid Marriage, of the dig:
ity which their reduced situation and Mr Dudley's
ing obliged to take orders for a Country Living
d so much lessened. They at once despised
Percivals ~~Petersons~~ as people of mean ~~no~~ family, and envied
m as people of fortune. They were jealous
their being more respected than themselves
d while they affected to consider them as of
Consequence, were continually seeking to lessen
m in the opinion of the Neighbourhood by
ndalous & Malicious reports. Such a family
this, was ill calculated to console Kitty for the
s of the Wynnes, or to fill up by their society
se occasionally irksome hours which in so retired
tuation would sometimes occur ~~[illegible]~~ for want of a
panion. Her aunt was most excessively fond
her, and miserable if she saw her for a moment

out of spirits; yet she lived in such constant appre
:hension of her marrying imprudently if she w
allowed the opportunity of Choosing, and was so diss
:fied with her behaviour when she saw her w
Young Men, for it was, from her natural d
:position remarkably open and unreserved, th
though she frequently wished for her Neice's sa
that the Neighbourhood were larger, and that s
had used herself to mix more with it, yet the
recollection of there being Young Men in almos
every Family in it, always conquered the Wish
The same fears that prevented Mrs Peterson
joining much in the Society of her Neighbou
led her equally to avoid inviting her relatio
to spend any time in her House - She had the
:fore constantly repelled the annual attemp
of a distant relation to visit her at Chetwyn
as there was a young Man in the Family of
whom she had heard many traits that alarme
her. This Son was however now on his trave
and the repeated solicitations of Kitty, joined

consciousness of having declined with too little
emony the frequent ~~endeavours~~ overtures of her Freinds
be admitted, and a real wish to see them her:
f, easily prevailed on her to press with great
nestness the pleasure of a visit from them during
Summer. Mr & Mrs Stanley were accordingly
come, and ~~Kitty~~ Catharine, in having an object to look
ward to, a something to expect that must
vitably relieve the dullness of a constant tete
te with her Aunt, was so delighted, and her spi:
ts so elevated, that for the three or four days im:
ediately preceding their Arrival, she could scarce
fix herself to any employment. In this point
rs. Percival always thought her defective, and
quently complained of a want of Steadiness
rseverance in her occupations, which were
no means congenial to the eagerness of Kitty's
isposition, and perhaps not often met with in
ny young person. The tediousness too of her
nt's conversation and the want of agreable
npanions greatly increased this desire of Chang
her Employments, for Kitty found herself much
oner tired of Reading, Working, or Drawing, in

Mrs Peterson's parlour than in her own Arbour
where Mrs Peterson for fear of its being damp,
never accompanied her.

As her Aunt prided herself on the c
propriety and Neatness with which every thi
in her Family was conducted, and had no high
satisfaction than that of knowing her house t
be always in complete Order, as her fortune
was good, and her Establishment Ample, fe
were the preparations Necessary for the rec
:tion of her Visitors. The day of their arrival
so long expected, at length ~~arrived~~ came, and the Noise of
the Coach & 4 as it drove round the sweep, wa
to Catherine a more interesting sound, than the
Music of an Italian Opera, which to most He
:roines is the hight of Enjoyment. Mr and Mrs
Stanley were people of Large Fortune & high
Fashion. He was a Member of the house of
Commons, and they were therefore most agreeab
necessitated to reside half the Year in Town; whe
Miss Stanley had been attended by the most capi
Masters from the time of her being six years old to

st Spring, which comprehending a period of twelve
ars had been dedicated to the acquirement of
complishments which were now to be displayed
d in a few Years entirely neglected. She was
~~[illegible]~~ [illegible] elegant in her appearance, ra:
ter handsome, and naturally not deficient in
bilities; but those Years which ought to have
en spent in the attainment of useful Know:
dge and Mental Improvement, had been all
stowed in learning Drawing, Italian and Music,
re especially the latter, and she now united to
se Accomplishments, an Understanding un:
improved by reading and a Mind totally devoi
ther of Taste or Judgement. Her temper was by
ture good, but unassisted by reflection, she had
ither patience under Disappointment, nor could
crifice her own inclinations to promote the happi:
ss of others. All her Ideas were towards the Elegan
her appearance, the fashion of her dress, and the
miration she wished them to excite. She professed
love of Books without Reading, was Lively with:
t Wit, and generally good humoured without Merit.

Such was Camilla Stanley; and Catherine, who
was prejudiced by her appearance, and who from
her solitary situation was ready to like anyone, t
her Understanding and Judgement would not o
:wise have been easily satisfied, felt almost c
:vinced, when she saw her, that Miss Stanley would be the very c
:panion she wanted, and in some degree mak
amends for the loss of Cecilia & Mary Wynne
She therefore attached herself to Camilla from t
first day of her arrival, and from being t
only young People in the house, they were by i
:clination constant Companions. Kitty was
:self a great reader, tho' perhaps not a very
deep one, and felt therefore highly delighted
find that Miss Stanley was equally fond of
Eager to know that their sentiments as to Book
were similar, she very soon began questioning
her new Acquaintance on the subject; but thoug
she was well read in Modern history herself, sh
chose rather to speak first of Books of a lighter
kind, of Books universally read and Admired.

~~-guments than any other of the same sort.~~

You have read Mrs Smith's Novels, I suppose?"
-d she to her Companion—. "Oh! Yes, replied the
-ter, and I am quite delighted with them—They
- the sweetest things in the world—" "And which
you prefer of them?" "Oh! dear, I think there
no comparison between them—Emmeline
so much better than any of the others—"
Many people think so, I know; but there does
t appear so great a disproportion in their Merits
me; do you think it is better written?"
h! I do not know anything about that—but
is better in ~~every~~ every thing— Besides, Ethelinde
so long—" "That is a very common Objection
-lieve, said Kitty, but for my own part, if
book is well written, I always find it too short."
o do I, only I get tired of it before it is finished."
ut did not you find the story of Ethelinde very in-
-teresting? And the Descriptions of Grasmere, are not
- Beautiful?" "Oh! I missed them all, because I
-as in such a hurry to know the end of it—Then
-om an easy transition she added, We are going to

the Lakes this Autumn, and I am quite mad with Joy; Sir Henry Devereux has promised to go with us, and that will make it so pleasant, you know—

"I dare say it will; but I think it is a pity that Sir Henry's powers of pleasing were not reserved for any occasion where they might be more wanted.— However I quite envy you the pleasure of such a tour."

"Oh! I am quite delighted with the thoughts of it; I can think of nothing else. I assure you I have done nothing for this last Month but plan what Cloathes I should take with me, and I have at last determined to take very few indeed besides my travelling Dress, and so I advise you to do, whenever you go; for I intend in case we should fall in with any races, or stop at Matlock or Scarborough, to have some Things made for the occasion."

"You intend then to go into Yorkshire?"

"I beleive not— indeed I know nothing of the Route, for I never trouble myself about such things—. I only know that we are to go from

rbyshire to Matlock and Scarborough, but to
hich of them first, I neither know nor care —
am in hopes of meeting some particular friends
mine at Scarborough — Augusta told me in her
st Letter that Sir Peter talked of going; but
en you know that is so uncertain. I cannot
ar Sir Peter, he is such a horrid Creature —"
He is, is he?" said Kitty, not knowing what else to say.
h! he is quite Shocking." Here the Conversation
as interrupted, and Kitty was left in a painful
Uncertainty, as to the particulars of Sir Peter's Cha:
racter; She knew only that he was Horrid and
Shocking, but why, and in what, yet remained
to be discovered. She could scarcely resolve what
think of her new Acquaintance; She appeared
be shamefully ignorant as to the Geography
England, if she had understood her right, and
equally devoid of Taste and Information. Kitty
as however unwilling to decide hastily; She
as at once desirous of doing Miss Stanley jus:
tice, and of having her own Wishes in her an:
swered; she determined therefore to suspend all

Judgement for some time. After supper, the Conver
:tion turning on the state of Affairs in the polit
World, Mrs P——, who was firmly of opinion
the whole race of Mankind were degenerating; s
that for her part, Everything she believed was g
:ing to rack and ruin, all order was destroyed o
the face of the World, The house of Commons she
did not break up sometimes till five in the
Morning, and Depravity never was so generall
:fore; concluding with a wish that she might li
to see the Manners of the People in Queen Elizabe
reign, restored again. "Well Ma'am, ~~said her Ne~~
~~[illegible]~~
~~[illegible]~~, but I hope you do not mean with the ti
to restore Queen Eliz:th herself."
"Queen Eliz:th, said Mrs Stanley who never hazar
a remark on History that was not well foun
lived to a good old age, and was a very Clever wo
"True Ma'am, said Kitty; but I do not consider
:ther of those Circumstances as meritorious in he
and they are very far from making me wish he

tum, for if she were to come again with the
ne abilities and the same good Constitution
might do as much Mischief and last as long
she did before — then turning to Camilla who
d been sitting very silent for some time, she
lded, What do you think of Elizabeth Miss
anley? I hope you will not defend her."
h! dear, said Miss Stanley, I know nothing of
litics, and cannot bear to hear them mentioned."
itty started at this repulse, but made no an:
wer; that Miss Stanley must be ignorant of
hat she could not distinguish from ~~History~~ Politics she
lt perfectly convinced. — She retired to her own
om, perplexed in her opinion about her new
quaintance, and fearful of her being very un:
ike Cecilia and Mary. She arose the next morn:
ing to experience a fuller conviction of this, and
ery future day encreased it. — She found no va:
iety in her conversation; She received no informa:
n from her but in fashions, and no Amusement
t in her performance on the Harpsichord; and

after repeated endeavours to find her what sh wished, she was obliged to give up the attemp and to consider it as fruitless. There had occasio:ly appeared a something like humour in Cam which had inspired her with hopes, that she mig at least have a natural Genius, tho' not an im:proved one, but these Sparklings of Wit happ so seldom, and were so ill-supported that she w at last convinced of their being merely accidenta All her stock of knowledge was exhausted in a very few Days, and when Kitty had learnt fr her, how large their house in Town was, whe the fashionable Amusements began, who were th celebrated Beauties and who the best Millener, Cam:la had nothing further to teach, except the Char:ters of any of her acquaintance as they occurre in Conversation, which was done with equal Ease and Brevity, by saying that the person was either the sweetest Creature in the world, and on of whom she was doatingly fond, or horrid, shock

d not fit to be seen.
s Catherine was very desirous of gaining every
sible information as to the Characters of the
lifax Family, and concluded that Miss Stanley
ust be acquainted with them, as she seemed to
so with every one of any Consequence, she took
opportunity as Camilla was one day enumerat-
ng all the people of rank that her Mother
isited, of asking her whether Lady Halifax
ere among the number.
h! Thank you for reminding me of her, she is
e sweetest Woman in the world, and one of
r most intimate Acquaintance; I do not
ppose there is a day passes during the six
onths that we are in Town, but what we see
h other in the course of it —. And I correspond
ith all the Girls."
They are then a very pleasant Family!" said
itty. They ought to be so indeed, to allow of such
equent Meetings, or all Conversation must be
t end."

"Oh! dear, not at all, said Miss Stanley, for som
:times we do not speak to each other for a
month together. We meet perhaps only in Pu
:lic, and then you know we are ~~not always~~ often not
able to get near enough; but in that case w
always nod & smile."

"Which does just as well — But I was going
ask you whether you have ever seen a Miss Wyn
with them?"

"I know who you mean perfectly — she wea
a blue hat — I have frequently seen her in Broo
Street, when I have been at Lady Halifax's Ba
She gives one every Month during the Winter —
But only think how good it is in her to tak
care of Miss Wynne, for she is a very distant
relation, and so poor that, as Miss Halifax to
me, her Mother was obliged to find her in Clo
Is not it shameful?" —

"That she should be so poor? it is indeed, with
such wealthy connexions as the Family have."

"Oh! no; I mean, was not it shameful in Mr Wy

have his Children so distressed. when he had
tually the Living of Chetwynde and two or three
racies, and only four Children to provide for. .
hat would he have done if he had had ten, as
ny people have?"
e would have given them all a good Education
d have left them all equally poor."
Well I do think there never was so lucky a
mily. Sir George Fitzgibbon you know sent
e eldest Girl to India entirely at his own
pence, where they say she is most nobly mar-
ied and the happiest Creature in the World —
dy Halifax you see has taken care of the young
st and treats her as if she were her Daughter;
he does not go out ~~into~~ Public with her to be
re; but then she is always present when her
dyship gives her Balls, and nothing can be
inder to her than Lady Halifax is; she would
ave taken her to Cheltenham last year, if there
ad been room enough at the Lodgings, and there-
re I dont think that <u>she</u> can have anything
complain of. Then there are the two Sons;

one of them the Bishop of M— has ~~sent to~~ got into
~~[illegible]~~ Army as a Lieutenant I suppose; and the
:ther is extremely well off I know, for I th
a notion that somebody puts him to School som
:where in Wales. Perhaps you knew them
when they lived here?"

"~~Slightly~~ Very well,: We met as often as your Family a
the Halifaxes do in Town, but as we seldom
any difficulty in getting near enough to speak
we seldom parted with merely a Nod & a Smile.
They were indeed a most charming Family, &
I believe have scarcely their Equals in the World,
The Neighbours we now have at the Parsonage, ap
:pear to more disadvantage in coming after them

"Oh! horrid Wretches! I wonder You can endure them

"Why, what would you have one do?"

"Oh! Lord, If I were in your place, I should abuse the
all day long."

"So I do, but it does no good."

"Well, I declare it is quite a pity that they should
be suffered to live. I wish my Father would propo

ocking all their Brains out, some day or other
en he is in the House. So abominably proud
their Family! And I dare say after all, that
e is nothing particular in it."

hy Yes, I believe they have reason to value them-
lves on it, if any body has; for you know he
Lord Amyatt's Brother."

h! I know all that very well, but it is no rea-
n for their being so horrid. I remember I met Miss
dley last Spring with Lady Amyatt at Ranelagh,
d she had such a frightful Cap on, that I have
er been able to bear any of them since. — And
you used to think the Wynnes very pleasant?"

ou speak as if their being so were doubtful!
easant! Oh! they were every thing that could in-
erest and Attach. It is not in my power to do
stice to their Merits, tho' not to feel them, I
ink must be impossible. They have unfitted
for any Society but their own!"

ell, That is just what I think of the Miss
alifaxes; by the bye, I must write to Caroline tomorrow, and I do not know what to say to her. The

~~[struck out]~~ two are just such other sweet Gir
but I wish Augusta's hair was not so dar
I cannot bear Sir Peter – Horrid Wretch! He
always laid up with the Gout, which is exc
:ingly disagreable to the Family."

"And perhaps not very pleasant to himself
But as to the Wynnes; do you really thin
them very fortunate?"

"Do I? Why, does not every body? Miss Halifa
& Caroline & Maria all say that they are the
luckiest Creatures in the World. So does Sir G
Fitzgibbon and so do Everybody."

"That is, Every body who have themselves con
:ferred an obligation on them. But do you
it lucky, for a Girl of Genius & Feeling to
sent in quest of a Husband to Bengal, to
married there to a Man of whose Disposition s
has no opportunity of judging till her Judgeme
is of no use to her, who may be a Tyrant, or a
or both for what she knows to the Contrary. D
you call that fortunate?"

know nothing of all that; I only know that
was extremely good in Sir George to fit her out
d pay her Passage, and that she would not have
und Many who would have done the same."
ish she had not found one, said Kitty with
eat Eagerness, she might then have remained in
ngland and been happy.
ell, I cannot conceive the hardship of going out
a very agreable Manner with two or three
eet Girls for Companions, having a delightful
yage to Bengal or Barbadoes or wherever it is,
d being married soon after one's arrival to
very charming Man immensely rich—. I see
hardship in all that."
Your representation of the Affair, said Kitty
ughing, certainly gives a very different idea
it from Mine. But supposing all this to be
ue, still, as it was by no means certain
at she would be so fortunate either in her voy
ge, her Companions, or her husband; in being o-
bliged to run the risk of their proving very

different, she undoubtedly experienced a great
hardship—. Besides, to a Girl of any Delicacy, the
voyage in itself, since the object of it is so univers
known, is a punishment that needs no other
to make it very severe."

"I do not see that at all. She is not the first G
who has gone to the East Indies for a Husband,
I declare I should think it very good fun, if I were a

"I beleive you would think very differently then
But at least you will not defend her Sister's s
:tuation? Dependant even for her Cloathes on the
bounty of others, who of course do not pity
as by your own account, they consider her as
fortunate."

"You are extremely nice upon my word; Lad
Halifax is a delightful Woman, and one of the
sweetest tempered Creatures in the World; I am
I have every reason to speak well of her, for w
are under most amazing Obligations to her. Sh
has frequently chaperoned me when my Mother
been indisposed, and last Spring she lent me h

on horse three times, which was a prodigious
vour, for it is the most beautiful Creature
hat ever was seen, and I am the only person
e ever lent it to.
~~If so, Mary Wynne can receive very little ad:~~
~~vantage from her having it."~~
continued she,
and then, the Miss Halifaxes are quite delightful. Maria is one of the cleverest Girls that
ever were known - Draws in Oils, and plays
anything by sight. She promised me one of her
rawings before I left Town, but I entirely forgot
ask her for it. I would give anything to have one."
~~bly indeed, if Maria will give [illegible] drawing~~
~~ing she can have nothing to complain of but~~
~~she does not write in spirits, I suppose she~~
~~has not yet been fortunate enough to be quite~~
~~reconciled~~. "But was not it very odd" said Kitty, "that
e Bishop should send Charles Wynne to sea, when
must have had a much better chance of providing for him in the Church, which was the pro:
fession that Charles liked best, and the one for
hich his Father had intended him? The Bishop

I know had often promised Mr Wynne a living,
as he never gave him one, I think it was in-
:cumbent on him to transfer the promise to
son."
"I believe you think he ought to have resigned
Bishopric to him; you seem determined to be dis-
:satisfied with every thing that has been done for th
"Well, said Kitty, this is a subject on which
shall never agree, and therefore it will be use
to continue it farther, or to mention it again
She then left the room, and running out of the
House was soon in her dear Bower where she
could indulge in peace all her affectionate Ang
against the relations of the Wynnes, which wa
greatly heightened by finding from Camilla tha
they were in general considered as having ac
particularly well by them -. She amused herself
for some time in Abusing, and Hating them
all, with great spirit, and when this tribute
her regard for the Wynnes, was paid, and the
:er began to have its usual influence over h

irits. she contributed towards settling them, by
king out a book, for she had always one about
, and reading. She had been so employed for
rly an hour, when Camilla came running to:
ards her with great Eagerness, and apparently great
asure. "Oh! my Dear Catherine, said she, half
t of Breath — I have such delightful News for
— But you shall guess what it is — We
e the happiest Creatures in the World; would
believe it, the Dudleys have sent us an in:
itation to a Ball at their own House. What
arming People they are! I had no idea of there
ing so much sense in the whole Family —
eclare I quite doat upon them. And it hap:
ens so fortunately too, for I expect a new Cap
m Town tomorrow which will just do for a
ll Gold Net — It will be a most angelic thing — Every
dy will be longing for the pattern." The ex:
ectation of a Ball was indeed very agreable
telligence to Kitty, who fond of Dancing and seldom
le to enjoy it, had reason to feel even greater

pleasure in it than her Freind; for to her, it w
now no novelty.. Camilla's delight however w
by no means inferior to Kitty's, and she ra
expressed the most of the two. The Cap came a
every other preparation was soon completed; w
these were in agitation the Days passed gaily
:way, but when Directions were no longer n
:cessary, Taste could no longer be displayed, a
Difficulties no longer overcome, the short pe
that intervened before the day of the Ball h
heavily on their hands, and every hour was t
long. The very few Times that Kitty had e
enjoyed the Amusement of Dancing was an e
:cuse for her impatience, and an apology
the Idleness it occasioned to a Mind natural
very active; but her Freind without such a
was infinitely worse than herself. She could d
nothing but wander from the house to the G
:den, and from the Garden to the avenue, w
:dering when Thursday would come, which she
might easily have ascertained, and counting th

urs as they passed which served only to lengthen
m.—. They retired to their rooms in high
irits on Wednesday night, but Kitty awoke the
xt Morning with a violent Toothake. It was in
in that she endeavoured at first to deceive
self; her feelings were witnesses too acute
it's reality; with as little success did she try
sleep it off, for the pain she suffered prevent:
d her closing her Eyes—. She then summoned
r Maid and with the Assistance of the House:
eeper, every remedy that the receipt book or
e head of the latter contained, was tried, but in:
ffectually; for though for a short time relieved
them, the pain still returned. She was now
liged to give up the endeavour, and to reconcile
self not only to the pain of a Toothake, but
the loss of a Ball; and though she had with
much eagerness looked forward to the day of its
rival, had received such pleasure in the necessary
eparations, and promised herself so much delight
it, Yet she was not so totally void of philosophy

as many Girls of her age, might have bee
in her Situation. She considered that there
Misfortunes of a much greater magnitude than
loss of a Ball, experienced every day by some
of Mortality, and that the time might come when S
would herself look back with Wonder and perha
with Envy on her having known no greater ve
:tion. By such reflections as these, she soon re
:soned herself into as much Resignation & Pat
as the pain she suffered, would allow of, whi
after all was the greatest Misfortune of the tw
and told the sad story when she entered the Brea
:fast room, with tolerable Composure. Mrs ~~P~~ Percival
more grieved for her toothake than her disappoin
:ment, as she feared that it would not be possible
prevent her Dancing with a Man if she went
was eager to try everything that had already
been applied to alleviate the pain, while at
same time She declared it was impossible fo
her to leave the House. Miss Stanley who join
to her concern for her Friend, felt a mixture

rad lest her Mother's proposal that they should
e remain at home, might be accepted, was
y violent in her sorrow on the occasion, and
ough her apprehensions on the subject were soon
ieted by Kitty's protesting that sooner than allow
y one to stay with her, she would herself go, she
tinued to lament it with such unceasing ve:
mence as at last drove Kitty to her own room.
r Fears for herself being now entirely dissipated
t her more than ever at leisure to pity and
secute her Friend who tho' safe when in her
n room, was frequently removing from it to
me other in hopes of being more free from pain;
d then had no opportunity of escaping her—.
be sure, there never was anything so shocking,
d Camilla; To come on such a day too! For one
uld not have minded it you know had it
en at *any other* time. But it always is so.
ever was at a Ball in my Life, but what
mething happened to prevent somebody from
ing! I wish there were no such things as Teeth
the World; they are nothing but plagues to

one, and I dare say, that People might easily in
something to eat with instead of them; Poor Th
what pain you are in! I declare it is quite sho
:ing to look at you. But you wont have it out w
you? For Heaven's sake dont; for there is noth
I dread so much. I declare I had rather undergo
greatest Tortures in the World than have a too
drawn. Well! how patiently you do bear it! ho
can you be so quiet? Lord, if I were in your pl
I should make such a fuss, there would be no
:ing one. I should torment you to Death."

"So you do, as it is." thought Kitty.

"For my own part, Catherine said Mrs ~~Peterson~~ Percival
I have not a doubt but that you caught this
toothake by sitting so much in that Arbour, for
is always damp. I know it has ruined your
Constitution entirely; and indeed I do not believ
it has been of much service to mine; I sate d
in it last May to rest myself, and I have ne
been quite well since —. I shall order John to p
it all down I assure you."

"I know you will not do that Ma'am, said Kitty.

u must be convinced how unhappy it would
ke me."
talk very ridiculously Child; it is all whim &
nsense. Why cannot you fancy this room an Arbour?"
ad this room been built by Cecilia & Mary, I should
e valued it equally Ma'am, for it is not merely
name of an Arbour, which charms me."
ly indeed Mrs ~~P~~ [Percival], said Mrs Stanley, I must
k that Catherine's affection for her Bower is the
ct of a sensibility that does her Credit. I love
ee a Freindship between young ~~Ladies~~ [Persons] and alway
sider it as a sure mark ~~of their being disposed~~ [of an amiable]
~~to each other~~ [affectionate disposition]. I have from Camilla's infancy
ght her to think the same, and have taken
at pains to introduce her to young people of her
age who were likely to be worthy of her regard.
~~e is something mighty pretty I think in young~~
~~corresponding with each other, and~~ nothing
ms the taste more than sensible & Elegant Let:
s—. Lady Halifax thinks just like me—Camilla
esponds with her Daughters, and I beleive I may
ture to say that they are none of them the worse for it."
se ideas were too modern to suit Mrs ~~P~~ [Percival] who

considered a correspondence between Girls as pro
:tive of no good, and as the frequent origin of
:prudence & Error by the effect of pernicious ad
and bad Example. She could not therefore refra
from saying that for her part, she had lived fif
Years in the world without having ever had a co
:pondent, and did not find herself at all the
respectable for it— Mrs Stanley could say noth
in answer to this, but her Daughter who wa
less governed by Propriety, said in her thought
way, "But who knows what you might hav
been Ma'am, if you had had a Correspondent
perhaps it would have made you quite a diff
Creature. I declare I would not be without tho
I have for all the World. It is the greatest
:light of my Life, and you cannot think how
their Letters have formed my taste as Mama
says, for I hear from them generally every w
"You received a Letter from Augusta Barlow to day, did no
my Love? said her Mother— She writes remark
well I know."

"Oh! Yes Ma'am, the most delightful Letter you ever heard of. She sends me a long account of the new ~~Dress~~ [Regency walking dress] Lady Susan has given her, and it is so beautiful that I am quite dieing with envy for it." "Well, I am prodigiously happy to hear such pleasing news of my young friend; I have a high regard for Augusta, and most sincerely partake in the general Joy on the occasion. But does she say nothing else? it seemed to be a long Letter—Are they to be at Scarborough?" "Oh! Lord, she never once mentions it, now I recollect it; and I entirely forgot to ask her when I wrote last. She says nothing indeed except about the ~~Dress~~ [Regency]." "She must write well thought Kitty, to make a long Letter upon a ~~Jacket and petticoat~~ [Bonnet & Pelisse]." She then left the room tired of listening to a conversation which tho' it might have diverted her had she been well, served only to fatigue and depress her, while in pain. Happy was it for her, when the hour of dressing came, for Camilla satisfied with being surrounded by her Mother and half the Maids in the House did not want her assistance, and was

too agreeably employed to want her Society. She
remained therefore alone in the parlour, till j
by Mr Stanley & her Aunt, who however afte
a few enquiries, allowed her to ~~remain~~ continue undistu
:ed and began their usual conversation on Poli
This was a subject on which they could neve
agree, for Mr Stanley who considered himself
perfectly qualified by his Seat in the House, to de
on it without hesitation, resolutely maintai
that the Kingdom had not for ages been in so
flourishing & prosperous a state, and Mrs ~~Pe~~ Percic
with equal warmth, tho' perhaps less argumen
as vehemently asserted that the whole Natio
would speedily be ruined, and everything as she
expressed herself be at sixes & sevens. It was n
however unamusing to Kitty to listen to the
Dispute, especially as she began then to be m
free from pain, and without taking any sha
in it herself, she found it very entertaining to
observe the eagerness with which they both defe
their opinions, and could not help thinking th

r Stanley would not feel more disappointed
her Aunt's expectations were fulfilled, than her
nt would be mortified by their failure. After
iting a considerable time Mrs Stanley & her daug
appeared, and Camilla in high Spirits, & per:
t good humour with her own looks, was more
lent than ever in her lamentations over her
iend as she practised her scotch Steps about
room.— At length they departed, & Kitty better
e to amuse herself than she had been the whole
y before, wrote a long account of her Misfortunes
Mary Wynne. When her Letter was concluded
had an opportunity of witnessing the truth of
t assertion which says that Sorrows are lightened
Communication, for her toothake was then so
ch releived that she began to entertain an
a of following her Friends to Mr Dudley's. They
d been gone ~~but half~~ an hour, and as every thing
ative to her Dress was in complete readiness,
considered that in ~~an hour & a half~~ another hour since there
s so little a way to go, she might be there.—
y were gone in Mr Stanley's Carriage and therefore

she might follow in her Aunts. As the plan se
:ed so very easy to be executed, and promise
so much pleasure, ~~[illegible]~~ it was after a fe
Minutes deliberation finally adopted, and runn
up stairs, she rang in great haste for her Ma
The Bustle & Hurry which then ensued for nea ~~[illegible]~~
an hour was at last happily concluded by he
finding herself very well-dressed and in hig
Beauty. ~~Nanny~~ Anne was then dispatched in th
same haste to order the Carriage, while her M
:tress was putting on her gloves, & arranging t
folds of her dress, ~~and pursuing herself with~~
~~[illegible]~~. In a few Minutes she hear
the Carriage drive up to the Door, and tho' a
first surprised at the expedition with which
had been got ready, she concluded after a litt
reflection that the Men had received some h
of her intentions beforehand, and was hasten
out of the room, when ~~Nanny~~ Anne came running
:to it in the greatest hurry and agitation, e
:claimi

d Ma'am! Here's a Gentleman in a Chaise and
r come, and I cannot for my Life conceive who
is! I happened to be crossing the hall when
Carriage drove up, and — I knew nobody would
in the way to let him in but Tom, and he looks
awkward you know Ma'am, now his hair is just
e up, that I was not willing the gentleman
ld see him, and so I went to the door myself.
d he is one of the handsomest young Men you
ld wish to see; I was almost ashamed of being
in my Apron Ma'am
n ~~because you know Ma'am I [illegible] all [illegible] up for~~
, but however he is vastly handsome and did
seem to mind it at all.- And he asked me
ether the Family were at home; and so I said
rybody was gone out but you Ma'am, for I
ld not deny you because I was sure you would
to see him. And then he asked me whether
and Mrs Stanley were not here, and so I said
, and then —
d Heavens! said Kitty, what can all this mean!
who can it possibly be! Did you never see him
fore? And Did not he tell you his Name?"

"No Ma'am, he never said anything about it— then I asked him to walk into the parlour, an was prodigious agreable, and—

"Whoever he is, said her Mistress, he has m a great impression upon you Nanny—But did he come from? and what does he want h

"Oh! Ma'am, I was going to tell you, that I fan his business is with you; for he asked me w :ther you were at leisure to see anybody, an desired I would give his Compliments to you, say he should be very happy to wait on yo However I thought he had better not come into your Dressing room, especially as everyth is in such a litter, so I told him if he wou be so obliging as to stay in the parlour, I w run up stairs and tell you he was come, a I dared to say that you would wait upon <u>him</u> Lord Ma'am, I'd lay anything that he is come to ask you to dance with him tonight, & ha got his Chaise ready to take you to Mr Dudley

Kitty could not help laughing at this idea

nly wished it might be true, as it was very
-kely that she would be too late for any other part-
r — "But what in the name of wonder, can
have to say to me? Perhaps he is come to
the house - he comes in stile at least; and
will be some consolation for our losses to be
-bed by a Gentleman in a chaise & 4 - What
-ery has his servants?"
Why that is the most wonderful thing about
im Ma'am, for he has not a single servant
th him, and came with hack horses; But he
as handsome as a Prince for all that, and has
-ite the look of one - Do dear Ma'am, go down, for
m sure you will be delighted with him -"
-ell, I believe I must go; but it is very odd!
hat can he have to say to me." Then giving
look at herself in the Glass, she walked
ith great impatience, tho' trembling all the
-hile from not knowing what to expect, down
-irs, and after pausing a moment at the door
gather Courage for opening it, she resolutely
entered the room.

The Stranger, whose appearance did not disg
the account she had received of it from her Ma
rose up on her entrance, and laying aside the
Newspaper he had been reading, advanced tow
her with an air of the most perfect Ease & Vi
:city, and said to her, "It is certainly a very aw
:ward circumstance to be thus obliged to intr
:duce myself, but I trust that the necessity
the case will plead my Excuse, and prevent
your being prejudiced by it against me.- Your
name, I need not ask Ma'am-. ~~Miss Peterson~~ Miss Percival
too well known to me by description to need
information of that." Kitty, who had been ex
:pecting him to tell his own name, instead
hers, and who from having been little in com
:pany, and never before in such a situation, felt
herself unable to ask it, tho' she had been
planning her speech all the way down stairs, w
so confused & distressed by this unexpected addre
that she could only return a slight curtesy to
and accepted the chair he reached her, without

nowing what she did. The gentleman then continued
u are, I dare say, surprised to see me returned
m France so soon, and nothing indeed but bu:
iness could have brought me to England; a very
lancholy affair has now occasioned it, and I
s unwilling to leave it without paying my
pects to the Family in Devonshire whom I
ve so long wished to be acquainted with—."
tty, who felt much more surprised at his
pposing her to be so, than at seeing a person
England, whose having ever left it was per:
tly unknown to her, still continued silent
m wonder & Perplexity, and her visitor still
tinued to talk. "You will suppose Madam
t I was not the less desirous of waiting
you, from your having Mr & Mrs Stanley with
.. I hope they are well? and Mrs ~~P~~ Percival,
does she do?" Then without waiting for an
swer he gaily added, "But my dear Miss Per
cival
~~—~~ you are going out I am sure; and I am
taining you from your appointment. How

can I ever expect to be forgiven for such injur
Yet how can I, so circumstanced, forbear to offe
You seem dressed for a Ball? But this is the La
of gaiety I know; I have for many years been
desirous of visiting it. You have Dances I su
:ppose at least every week – But where ar
the rest of your party gone, and what kind
:gel in compassion to me, has excluded you
from it?"
"Perhaps Sir, said Kitty extremely confused b
his manner of speaking to her, and highly
:pleased with the freedom of his conversatio
towards one who had never seen him bef
and did not now know his name, " perha
Sir, you are acquainted with Mr & Mrs Stan
and your business may be with them?"
"You do me too much honour Ma'am, replied
Laughing, in supposing me to be acquainted
Mr & Mrs Stanley; I merely know them by sigh
very distant relations; only my Father & Mot

thing more I assure you."

racious Heaven! said Kitty, are you Mr Stanley
en?—I beg a thousand pardons—Though
lly upon recollection I do not know for what
you never told me your name—

beg your pardon—I made a very fine speech
en you entered the room, all about introduc:
ig myself; I assure you it was very great
r me."

he speech had certainly great Merit, said Kitty
iling; I thought so at the time; but ~~as~~ since you
ver mentioned your name in it, as an intro:
uctory one it might have been better."

here was such an air of good humour and
iety in Stanley, that Kitty, tho' perhaps not
thorized to address him with so much fami:
iarity on so short an acquaintance, could
t forbear indulging the natural Unreserved
Vivacity of her own Disposition, in speaking
him, as he spoke to her. She was intimately
quainted too with his Family who were her re:

:lations, and she chose to consider herself entitle
by the connexion to forget how little a while
had known each other. "Mr & Mrs Stanley & yo
Sister are extremely well, said she, and will
dare say be very much surprised to see you
But I am sorry to hear that your return to Eng
has been occasioned by any unpleasant circum
"Oh! Dont talk of it, said he, it is a most confou
shocking affair, & makes me miserable to thin
of it; But where are my Father & Mother, & yo
Aunt gone? Oh! Do you know that I met the p
:tiest little waiting maid in the World, when
came here; she let me into the house; I took
for you at first."
"You did me a great deal of honour, and give m
more credit for good nature than I deserve, for
<u>never</u> go to the door when any one comes."
"Nay dont be angry; I mean no offence. But
me, where are you going to so smart? Your car
is just coming round."
"I am going to a Dance at a Neighbour's, ~~of ...~~ w

r Family and my Aunt are already gone." ~~79~~ 41
ne, without you! what's the meaning of that?
t I suppose you are like myself, rather long
dressing."
must have been so indeed, if that were the
se for they have been gone nearly these two
urs; The reason however was not what
u suppose - I was prevented going by a pain-
By a pain! interrupted Stanley, Oh! heavens,
t is dreadful indeed! No Matter where the pain
s. But my dear Miss ~~Peterson~~ Percival, what do you
y to my accompanying you? And suppose
u were to dance with me too? I think it
uld be very pleasant."
can have no objection to either I am sure, said
itty laughing to find how near the truth her
aid's conjecture had been; on the contrary I shall
highly honoured by both, and I can answer for
r being extremely welcome to the Family who
e the Ball."
! hang them; who cares for that; they cannot
n me out of the house. But I am afraid I

shall cut a sad figure among all your Devons Beaux in this dusty, travelling apparel, and I not wherewithal to change it. You can procure me powder perhaps, and I must get a pair of Sho from one of the men, for I was in such a devil a hurry to leave Lyons that I had not time have anything packed up but some linen." Kitty readily undertook to procure for him every thi he wanted, & telling the footman to shew him Mr Stanley's dressing room, gave Nanny orders send in some powder & pomatum, which orde Nanny chose to execute in person. As Stanley's :parations in dressing were confined to such v trifling articles, Kitty of course expected him about ten minutes; but she found that it ha not been merely a boast of vanity in saying he was dilatory in that respect, as he kept waiting for him above half an hour, so that Clock had struck ten before he entered the ro and the rest of the party had gone by eight.

-ell, said he as he came in, have not I been very
-ick? I never hurried so much in my Life before."
"In that case you certainly have, replied Kitty,
all Merit you know is comparative."
"h! I knew you would be delighted with me for
-king so much haste—. But come, the Carriage
-eady; so, do not keep me waiting." And so say-
-g he took her by the hand, & led her out of the room.
-ky, my dear Cousin, said he when they were
-ted, this will be a most agreable surprize to
-y body to see you enter the room with such
smart Young Fellow as I am—I hope your Aunt
-t be alarmed."
"To tell you the truth, replied Kitty, I think the
-t way to prevent it, will be to send for her
-our Mother before we go into the room, especi-
-ly as you are a perfect Stranger, & must of course
introduced to Mr & Mrs Dudley—"
"! Nonsense, said he; I did not expect you to
-nd upon such Ceremony; Our acquaintance with
-h other renders all such Prudery, ridiculous;

Besides, if we go in together, we shall be the talk of the Country—

"To me replied Kitty, that would certainly b[e] most powerful inducement; but I scarcely kn[ow] whether my Aunt would consider it as such—. [Wo]:men at her time of life, have odd ideas of propriety [you] know."

"Which is the very thing that you ought to bre[ak] them of; and why should you object to enter[ing] a room with me where all our relations are, w[hen] you have done me the honour to admit me w[ith]:out any chaperone into your Carriage? Do not [you] think your Aunt will be as much offended [with] you for one, as for the other of these mighty c[rimes]"

"Why really said Catharine, I do not know bu[t] that she may; however, it is no reason tha[t] I should offend against Decorum a second tim[e] because I have already done it once."

"On the contrary, that is the very reason whic[h] makes it impossible for you to prevent it, s[ince]

n cannot offend for the first time again."
n are very ridiculous, said she laughing, but I
n afraid your arguments divert me too much
convince me."
t least they will convince you that I am very
uable, which after all, is the happiest con:
ition for me, and as to the affair of Propriety
e will let that rest till we arrive at our
rney's end—. This is a monthly Ball I suppose.
thing but Dancing here—."
I thought I had told you that it was given
a Mr Dudley—"
h! aye so you did; but why should not Mr Dudley
ve one every month! By the bye who is that
n? Every body gives Balls now I think; I
lieve I must give one myself soon—. Well, but
w do you like my Father & Mother? and poor
ttle Camilla too, has not she plagued you to
th with the Halifaxes?" Here the Carriage for:
nately stopped at Mr Dudley's, and Stanley was
o much engaged in handing her out of it, to wait

for an answer, or to remember that what he h
said required one. They entered the small vest
which Mr Dudley had raised to the Dignity of a
& Kitty immediately desired the footman who w
leading the way upstairs, to inform either Mrs
:terson, or Mrs Stanley of her arrival, & beg them
come to her, but Stanley unused to any contrad
& impatient to be amongst them, would neither
her to wait, or listen to what she said, & forcibly
:ing her arm within his, overpowered her voice w
the rapidity of his own, & Kitty half angry, &
laughing was obliged to go with him up stairs,
could even with difficulty prevail on him to re
:quish her hand before they entered the room. M
~~Peterson~~ Percival was at that very moment engaged
conversation with a Lady at the upper end of the
room, to whom she had been giving a long acc
of her Niece's unlucky disappointment, & the d
:ful pain that she had with so much fortitude,
the whole Day— "I left her however, said she, tha
heaven!, a little better, and I hope she has been a
to amuse herself with a book, poor thing! for sh

st otherwise be very dull. She is probably in
by this time, which while she is so poorly, is
best place for her you know Ma'am." The Lady
going to give her assent to this opinion, when
Noise of voices on the stairs, and the footman's
ning the door as if for the entrance of company,
acted the attention of every body in the room; and
it was in one of those Intervals between the
ces when every one seemed glad to sit down, Mrs
ison had a most unfortunate opportunity of
ing her Neice whom she had supposed in bed, or
using herself at the height of gaity with a
h, enter the room most elegantly dressed, with
mile on her Countenance, and a glow of mingled
rfulness & Confusion on her Cheeks, attended
a young Man uncommonly handsome, and
without any of her Confusion, appeared to
e all her vivacity. Mrs Percival colouring
t anger & astonishment, rose from her seat, &
ty walked eagerly towards her, impatient to
unt for what she saw appeared wonderful to
y body, and extremely offensive to her, while
nilla on seeing her Brother ran instantly to:

:wards him, and very soon explained who he wa[s]
her words & her actions. Mr Stanley, who so fondly
:ed on his son, that the pleasure of seeing him
after an absence of three Months prevented h[im]
feeling for the time any anger against him for
:turning to England without his knowledge, re[ceiv]
:ed him with equal surprise & delight; and so[on]
comprehending the cause of his Journey, forbor[e]
further conversation with him, as he was eage[r to]
see his Mother, & it was necessary that he sho[uld]
be introduced to Mr Dudley's family. This intr[oduc]
:tion to any one but Stanley would have been
:ly unpleasant, for they considered their dign[ity]
injured by his coming uninvited to their hou[se]
& received him with more than their usual h[aughti]
:ness: But Stanley who ~~joined to~~ with a vivaci[ty of]
temper seldom subdued, & a contempt of censu[re]
not to be overcome, possessed an opinion of his
Consequence, & a perseverance in his own schem[es]
which were not to be damped by the conduct [of]
others, appeared not to perceive it. The civili[ties]
therefore which they coldly offered, he received

gaity & ease peculiar to himself, and then at:
:ded by his Father & Sister walked into another
n where his Mother was playing at Cards, to
erience another Meeting, and undergo a repeti:
tion of pleasure, surprise, & Explanations. While
se were passing, Camilla eager to communicate
e she felt to some one who would attend to her,
urned to Catherine, & seating herself by her, im:
ediately began- "Well, did you ever know
ything so delightful as this? But it always
so; I never go to a Ball in my Life but what
nething or other happens unexpectedly that is
ite charming!"
Ball replied Kitty, seems to be a most eventful
ing to you-"
"Lord, it is indeed- But only think of my bro:
r's returning so suddenly- and how shocking
thing it is that has brought him over! I never
d any thing so dreadful-!"
hat is it pray that has occasioned his leaving
nce? I am sorry to find that it is a melan:
oly event."

"Oh! it is beyond anything you can conceive! H
favourite Hunter who was turned out in the p
on his going abroad, somehow or other fell ill —
I beleive it was an accident, but however it
something or other, or else it was something el
and so they sent an Express immediately to Lyo
where my Brother was, for they knew that h
:lued this Mare more than anything else in t
World besides; and so my Brother set off dire
for England, and without packing up anothe
Coat; I am quite angry with him about it; it
so shocking you know to come away without a chang
Cloathes—"

"Why indeed said Kitty, it seems to have been
very shocking affair from beginning to end."

"Oh! it is beyond anything You can conceive!
would rather have had *anything* happen to
that he should have lossed that mare."

"Except ~~your Brother's~~ his coming away without
other coat."

"Oh! yes, that has vexed me more than you ca

agine. — Well, & so Edward got to Brampton just
the poor Thing was dead; but as he could not
r to remain there *then*, he came off directly
Chetwynde on purpose to see us. — I hope he may
t go abroad again."

• you think he will not?"

! dear, to be sure he must, but I wish he may
t with all my heart. — You cannot think
o fond I am of him! By the bye are not you
love with him yourself?"

be sure I am replied Kitty laughing, I am
love with every handsome Man I see."

That is just like me — *I* am always in love
th every handsome Man in the world."

There you outdo me replied Catherine for I am
ly in love with those I *do* see." Mrs ~~Peterson~~ Percival
o was sitting on the other side of her, & who
gan now to distinguish the words, *Love* & *hand-
me Man*, turned hastily towards them, & said
hat are you talking of Catherine?" To which
therine immediately answered with the simple
ifice of a Child, "Nothing Ma'am." She had already

received a very severe lecture from her Aun
on the imprudence of her behaviour durin
the whole evening; she blamed her for com
to the Ball, for coming in the same Carriage w
Edward Stanley, and still more for entering th
room with him. For the last-mentioned offen
Catherine knew not what apology to give, an
tho' she longed in answer to the second to say tha
she had not thought it would be civil to mak
Mr Stanley *walk*, she dared not so to trifle wi
her aunt, who would have been but the more
:fended by it. The first accusation however she
:sidered as very unreasonable, as she thought
:self perfectly justified in coming. This conversa
continued till Edward Stanley entering the room
came instantly towards her, and telling her th
every one waited for *her* to begin the next Da
led her to the top of the room, for Kitty impati
to escape from so unpleasant a Companion, w
:out the least hesitation, or one civil scruple a
being so distinguished, immediately gave him
her hand, & joyfully left her seat. This Condu

wever was highly resented by several young
dies present, and among the rest by Miss Stanley
ose regard for her brother tho' *excessive*, & whose
ection for Kitty tho' *prodigious*, were not proof
ainst such an injury to her importance and
peace. Edward had however only consulted his
n inclinations in desiring Miss Peterson to begin
Dance, nor had he any reason to know that
was either wished or expected by anyone else
the Party. As an heiress she was certainly
consequence, but her Birth gave her no other
im to it, for her Father had been a Merchant.
was this very circumstance which rendered
is unfortunate affair so offensive to Camilla,
tho' she would sometimes boast in the pride
her heart, & her eagerness to be admired that
did not know who her grandfather had
n, and was as ignorant of everything rela
ive to Genealogy as to Astronomy, (and she might
ve added Geography) yet she was really proud
her family & Connexions, and easily offended
they were treated with Neglect. "I should not

have minded it, said she to her Mother, if she
been anybody else's daughter; but to see her p
:tend to be above me, when her Father wa
only a tradesman, is too bad! It is such an a
:front to our whole Family! I declare I thin
Papa ought to interfere in it, but he never
cares about anything but Politics. If I were
Pitt or the Lord Chancellor, he would take ca
I should not be insulted, but he never thin
about me; And it is so provoking that Edw
should let her stand there. I wish with all m
heart that he had never come to England!
hope she may fall down & break her neck,
sprain her Ancle." Mrs Stanley perfectly agr
with her daughter concerning the affair, & th
with less violence, expressed almost equal res
:ment at the indignity. Kitty in the meant
remained insensible of having given any one
:fence, and therefore unable either to offer an
:logy, or make a reparation; her whole atten
was occupied by the happiness she enjoyed i

ncing with the most elegant young Man in
e room, and every one else was equally un:
-garded. The Evening indeed to her, passed
delightfully; he was her partner during the
eatest part of it, and the united attractions that
possessed of Person, Address & vivacity, had easily
ined that preference from Kitty which they sel:
m fail of obtaining from every one. She was
happy to care either for her Aunt's ill humour
hich she could not help ~~observing~~ remarking, or for the
lteration in Camilla's behaviour which forced
self at last on her observation. Her Spirits were
vated above the influence of Displeasure in any
-, and she was equally indifferent as to the
use of Camilla's, or the continuance of her Aunt's.
ough Mr Stanley could never be really offended
any impudence or folly in his Son that had given him
pleasure of seeing him, ~~[illegible]~~ he was yet per:
ctly convinced that Edward ought not to re:
main in England, and was resolved to hasten his

leaving it as soon as possible; but when [he] talked to Edward about it, he found him much less dispos[ed] towards returning to France, than to accomp[any] them in their projected tour, which he assu[red] his Father would be infinitely more pleasa[nt] to him, and that as to the affair of travell[ing] he considered it of no importance, and wh[at] might be pursued at any little odd time, wh[en] he had nothing better to do. He advanced the[se] objections in a manner which plainly shew[ed] that he had scarcely a doubt of their being complied with, and appeared to consider his [Fa]:ther's arguments in opposition to them, as merely given with a view to keep up his a[u]:thority, & such as he should find little diff:iculty in combating. He concluded at last saying, as the chaise in which they return[ed] together from Mr Dudley's reached Mrs ~~Pe~~ Ripma[n's] "Well Sir, we will settle this point some ot[her] time, and fortunately it is of so little cons[equence]

-vence, that an immediate discussion of it is necessary." He then got out of the chaise & entered -house without waiting for his Father's Reply. was not till their return that Kitty could -unt for that coldness in Camilla's behaviour -her, which had been so pointed as to render impossible to be entirely unnoticed. When -wever they were seated in the Coach with two other Ladies, Miss Stanley's indignation -s no longer to be suppressed from breaking -t into words, & found the following vent. -ell, I must say this, that I never was at stupider Ball in my Life! But it always so; I am always disappointed in them for -ne reason or other. I wish there were no -ch things."

I am sorry Miss Stanley, said Mrs ~~Peterson~~ Percival drawing -rself up, that you have not been amused; every -ing was meant for the best I am sure, and it is a poor encouragement for your Mama to take -u to another if you are so hard to be satisfied."

"I do not know what you mean Ma'am about Mama's taking me to another. You know I a[m] come out."

"Oh! dear Mrs ~~P——t~~ Percival said Mrs Stanly, you mus[t] believe everything that my lively Camilla s[ays] for her spirits are prodigiously high sometimes, [and] she frequently speaks without thinking. I am s[ure] it is impossible for any one to have been at a more elegant or agreable dance, and so she wish[es] to express herself I am certain.

"To be sure I do, said Camilla very sulkily, onl[y] I must say that it is not very pleasant to ha[ve] any body behave so rude to one as to be quit[e] shocking! I am sure I am not at all offend[ed] and should not care if all the world were to stand above me, but still it is extremely ab:ominable, & what I cannot put up with. It [is] not that I mind it in the least, for I had ju[st] as soon stand at the bottom as at the top al[l] night long, if it was not so very disagreable. But to have a person come in, the middle of [...]

ning & take everybody's place is what I am not
d to, and tho' I do not care a pin about it myself,
sure you I shall not easily forgive or forget it."
is speech which perfectly explained the whole
air to Kitty, was shortly followed on her side
a very submissive apology, for she had too much
d Sense to be proud of her family, and too
ch good Nature to live at variance with any
. The Excuses she made, were delivered with
much real concern for the Offence, and such
affected Sweetness, that it was almost impossi:
le for Camilla to retain that anger which had
casioned them; she felt indeed most highly
atisfied to find that no insult had been intende
d that Catherine was very far from forgetting
difference in their birth for which she could
w only pity her, and her good humour being
tored with the same Ease in which it had been
ffected, she spoke with the highest delight of the
ening, & declared that she had never before been

at so pleasant a Ball. The same endeav
that had procured the forgiveness of Miss
ensured to her the cordiality of her Mother,
nothing was wanting but Mrs Pe[illegible]'s good
:mour to render the happiness of the others
:plete; but She, offended with Camilla for
affected Superiority, still more so with her b
:ther for coming to Chetwynde, & dissatisfied
the whole Evening, continued silent & Gloo
and was a restraint on the vivacity of
Companions. She eagerly seized the very fir
opportunity which ~~offered~~ the next Morni
offered to her/
of speaking to Mr Stanley on the subject o
his son's return, and after having expressed h
opinion of its being a very silly affair that
he came at all, concluded with desiring him
to inform Mr Edward Stanley that it was a
rule with her never to admit a young Ma
into her house as a visitor for any length of t

do not speak Sir, she continued, out of any
srespect to You; but I could not answer it to
self to allow of his stay; there is no know:
g what might be the consequence of it, if
were to continue here, for girls nowadays
ll always give a handsome young Man the
ference before any other, tho' for why, I never
ld discover, for what after all is Youth and
auty? ~~[illegible]~~ It
is ~~Young [illegible]~~ — ~~[illegible]~~ is but a
r substitute for real worth & Merit; Believe
Cousin that, what ever people may say
the contrary, there is certainly nothing like
tue for making us what we ought to be,
d as to a ~~[illegible]~~ young Man's, being
ung & handsome & having an agreable per:
n, it is nothing at all to the purpose for he
d much better be respectable. I always *did*
ike so, and I always *shall*, and therefore You

will oblige me very much by desiring your to leave Chetwynde, or I cannot be answerable what may happen between him and my Neice. You will be surprised to hear me say it, s continued, lowering her voice, but truth w out, and I must own that Kitty is one of t most impudent Girls that ever existed. ~~Her intimacies with Young Men are abominable and it is all the same to her, who it is, no comes amiss to her.~~ I assure you Sir, that I seen her sit and laugh and whisper with a young Man whom she has not seen above a dozen times. Her behaviour indeed is scan: lous, and therefore I beg you will send your away immediately, or everything will be at & Sevens." Mr Stanley who from one part of Speech had scarcely known to what length her insinuations of Kitty's impudence were meant to extend, now endeavoured to quiet h fears on the occasion, by assuring her, that on

ement he meant to allow only of his son's con:
tinuing that day with them, and that she
ight depend on his being more earnest in
affair from a wish of obliging her. He
dded also that he knew Edward to be very
sirous himself of returning to France, as he
isely considered all time lost that did not
ward the plans in which he was at pre:
nt engaged, tho' he was but too well con:
inced of the contrary himself. His assuranc
some degree quieted Mrs P——, & left her
lerably relieved of her Cares & Alarms, & better
isposed to behave with civility towards his Son
ring the short remainder of his stay at Chet:
ynde. Mr Stanley went immediately to Ed:
ard, to whom he repeated the Conversation tha
d passed between Mrs P—— & himself, &
ngly pointed out the necessity of his leaving
tnynde the next day, since his word was
eady engaged for it. His son however appeared
uck only by the ridiculous apprehensions of

Mrs Peterson; and highly delighted at having
:casioned them himself, seemed engrossed al
in thinking how he might increase them
without attending to any other part of his Fa
:ther's Conversation. Mr Stanley could get no d
:minate Answer from him, and tho' he still hoped for
best, they parted almost in anger on his side
His Son though by no means disposed to ma
rany otherwise attached to Miss ~~Peterson~~ Percival tha
as a good natured lively Girl who seemed ple
with him, took infinite pleasure in alarm
the jealous fears of her aunt by his attentio
to her, without considering what effect the
might have on the Lady herself. He would a
:ways sit by her when she was in the room
appeared dissatisfied if she left it, and was
first to enquire whether she meant som
return. He was delighted with her Drawin
and enchanted with her performance on
Harpsichord; Everything that she said, appea
to interest him; his Conversation was addres

her alone, and she seemed to be the sole ob:
t of his attention. That such efforts should
ceed with one so tremblingly alive to every
m of the kind as Mrs ~~P[illegible]~~ Percival, is by no means
natural, and that they should have equal in:
uence with her Niece whose imagination was
ly, and whose Disposition romantic, who
s already extremely pleased with him, and of
rse desirous that he might be so with her,
as little to be wondered at. Every moment
it added to the conviction of his liking her,
de him still more pleasing, and strengthend
her Mind a wish of knowing him better.
for Mrs ~~P[illegible]~~ ercival, she was in tortures the whole
; Nothing that she had ever felt before on a
milar occasion was to be compared to the sen:
tions which then distracted her; her fears had
er been so strongly, or indeed so reasonably ex:
ed. ~~before~~ Her dislike of Stanly, her anger at her
e, her impatience to have them separated
quered every idea of propriety & Goodbreeding,

and though he had never mentioned any inten of leaving them the next day, she could not help asking him after Dinner, in her eagerness to h him gone, at what time he meant to set ou "Oh! Ma'am, replied he, if I am off by twelve night, you may think yourself lucky; and if am not, you can only blame yourself for ha left so much as the <u>hour</u> of my departure my own disposal." Mrs ~~Peterson~~ Percival coloured very highly at this speech, and without addressin herself to any one in particular, immediate began a long harangue on the shocking beh :viour of modern young Men, & the wonderfu alteration that had taken place in them, s her time, which she illustrated with man instructive anecdotes of the Decorum & Mode which had marked the Characters of those w he had known, when she had been young. T however did not prevent his walking in th

rden with her Neice, without any other com:
nion for nearly an hour in the course of the
ning. They had left the room for that pur:
se with Camilla at a time when Mrs Peterson
d been out of it, nor was it for some time
ter her return to it, that she could discover
ere they were. Camilla had taken two or three
ns with them in the walk which led to
e Arbour, but soon growing tired of listening
a Conversation in which she was seldom
ited to join, & from its turning occasionally
Books, very little able to do it, she left them
ther in the Arbour,
wander alone to some other part of the
rden, to eat the fruit, & examine Mrs Peter:
n's Greenhouse. Her absence was so far from
ing regretted, that it was scarcely noticed
them, & they continued conversing together
almost every subject, for Stanley seldom
welt long on any, and had something to say
all, till they were interrupted by her Aunt.

Kitty was by this time perfectly convin
that both in Natural Abilities, & acquired
:formation, Edward Stanley was infinitely
:perior to his Sister. Her desire of knowing
he was so, had induced her to take every o
:portunity of turning the Conversation on H
and they were very soon engaged in an his
:rical dispute, for which no one was mor
calculated than Stanley who was so far from be
really of any party, that he had scarcely a
:ed opinion on the Subject. He could therefo
always take either side, & always argue w
temper. In his indifference on all such top
he was very unlike his Companion, wh
judgement being guided by her feelings wh
were eager & warm, was easily decided, an
though it was not always infallible, she
:fended it with a Spirit & Enthousiasm w
marked her own reliance on it. They h
continued therefore for sometime conversi

this manner on the character of Richard
3d, which he was warmly defending
[illegible] he suddenly seized hold of her hand, and
[illegible]laiming with great emotion, "Upon my honour
[illegible] are entirely mistaken", pressed it passio:
[illegible]ately to his lips, & ran out of the arbour.
[illegible]tonished at this behaviour, for which she
[illegible]s wholly unable to account, she continued
[illegible] a few Moments motionless on the seat
[illegible]here he had left her, and was then on the
[illegible]nt of following him up the narrow
[illegible]lk through which he had passed, when on
[illegible]king up the one that lay immediately
[illegible]ore the arbour, she saw her Aunt walking
[illegible]wards her with more than her usual quick:
[illegible]ess. This explained at once the reason of
[illegible] leaving her, but his leaving her in such
[illegible]anner was rendered still more inexplicable
[illegible] it. She felt a considerable degree of confusion
[illegible] having been seen by her in such a place

with Edward, and at having that part of h
conduct, for which she could not herself acc
witnessed by one to whom all gallantry w
odious. She remained therefore confused distr
& irresolute, and suffered her Aunt to approa
her, without leaving the Arbour. Mrs ~~Pet~~ Perciv
looks were by no means calculated to anim
the spirits of her Neice, who in silence awa
her accusation, and in silence meditated he
Defence. After a few Moments suspence, for
Peterson was too much fatigued to speak im
:mediately, she began with great Anger a
Asperity, the following harangue. "Well; th
is beyond anything I could have supposed.
:fligate as I knew you to be, I was not pr
:pared for such a sight. This is beyond any
you ever did before; beyond any thing I ever he
of in my Life! Such Impudence, I never
witnessed before in such a Girl! And thi

he reward for all the cares I have taken in
ur Education; for all my troubles & Anxieties;
d Heaven knows how many they have
een! All I wished for, was to breed you up
iteously; I never wanted you to play upon
e Harpsichord, or draw better than any one
lse; but I had hoped to see you respectable
d good; to see you able & willing to give
n example of Modesty and Virtue to the
ung people here abouts. I bought you Blair's
rmons, and ~~Seccar's explanation of the Catechism~~ Coelebs in Search of a Wife,
gave you the key to my own Library, and
rrowed a great many good books of my
ighbours for you, all to this purpose. But
might have spared myself the trouble—
! Catherine, you are an abandoned Creature,
d I do not know what will become of you.
am glad however, she continued softening into
me degree of Mildness, to see that you have

some shame for what you have done, an
if you are really sorry for it, and your futu
life is a life of penitence and reformation
perhaps you may be forgiven. But I plai
see that every thing is going to sixes & seven
and all order will soon be at an end throughou
the Kingdom."

"Not however Ma'am the sooner, I hope, from
any conduct of mine, said Catharine in a ton
of great humility, for upon my honour I ha
done nothing this evening that can contri
to overthrow the establishment of the kingdo
"You are Mistaken Child, replied she; the we
:fare of every Nation depends upon the virt
of it's individuals, and any one who offends in
gross a manner against decorum & propri
is certainly hastening it's ruin. You have b
giving a bad example to the World, and th
World is but too well disposed to receive su

ardon me Madam, said her Neice; but I am
ve given an Example only to You, for You
ne have seen the offence. Upon my word
wever, there is no danger to fear from what
ave done; Mr Stanley's behaviour has given
as much surprise, as it has done to You,
d I can only suppose that it was the effect
his high spirits, authorized in his opinion
our relationship. But do you consider Ma:
am that it is growing very late? Indeed
had better return to the house." This
eech as she well knew, would be unanswer:
ble with her Aunt, who instantly rose, and
rried away under so many apprehensions
her own health, as banished for the time
e anxiety about her Neice, who walked qui:
tly by her side, revolving within her own Mind
occurrence that had given her Aunt so much
arm. "I am astonished at my own imprudence,
id Mrs ~~Peterson~~ Percival; How could I be so forgetful as to

sit down out of doors at such a time of n
I shall certainly have a return of my rheum
:tism after it - I begin to feel very chill alre
I must have caught a dreadful cold by the
time - I am sure of being lain-up all the
:ter after it - " Then reckoning with her fing
"Let me see; This is July; the cold weather w
soon be coming in - August - September - O
:ber - November - December - January - Februar
March - April - Very likely I may not be tole
again before May. I must and will have that
:bour pulled down - it will be the death of m
who knows *now*, but what I may never
:cover - Such things *have* happened - My
:ticular friend Miss Sarah Hutchinson's death
occasioned by nothing more - She staid out la
one Evening in April, and got wet through
for it rained very hard, and never changed
Cloathes when she came home - It is unk
how many people have died in consequence
catching Cold! I do not believe there is a dis

the World except the Small pox which does
t spring from it." It was in vain that Kitty
deavoured to convince her that her fears on
e occasion were groundless; that it was not
t late enough to catch cold, and that even if it
re, she might hope to escape any other com:
plaint, and to recover in less than ten Months.
rs ~~Peterson~~ Percival only replied that she hoped she knew
re of Ill health than to be convinced in such
point by a Girl who had always been perfectly
ll, and hurried up stairs leaving Kitty to
ke her apologies to Mr & Mrs Stanley for going
bed —. Tho' Mrs ~~Peterson~~ Percival seemed perfectly satis:
ied with the goodness of the apology herself, yet
itty felt somewhat embarrassed to find that
e only one she could offer to their Visitors was
at her Aunt had *perhaps* caught cold, for
rs Peterson charged her to make light of it, for
ar of alarming them. Mr & Mrs Stanley however
ho well knew that their Cousin was easily
rified on that Score, received the account of it

with very little surprise, and all proper c
:cern. Edward & his Sister soon came in, & K
had no difficulty in gaining an explanation of his Conduct f
him, for he was too warm on the subject h
:self, and too eager to learn its success, to ref
from making immediate Enquiries about it;
she could not help feeling both surprised & off
:ed at the ease & Indifference with which he
owned that all his intentions had been to fr
:en her Aunt by pretending an affection for
a design so very incompatible with that par
:ality which she had at one time been alm
convinced of his feeling for her. It is true tha
she had not yet seen enough of him to be a
:tually in love with him, yet she felt grea
disappointed that so handsome, so elegant, s
lively a young Man should be so perfectly f
from any such Sentiment as to make it
principal Sport. There was a Novelty in his
:racter which to her was extremely pleasa

[hi]s person was uncommonly fine, his Spirits & [viv]acity suited to her own, and his Manners [at] once so animated & insinuating, that she [tho]ught it must be impossible for him to be [ot]herwise than amiable, and was ready to give him [cre]dit for being ~~exceptionably~~ perfectly so. He knew the [po]wers of them himself; to them he had often [bee]n indebted for his father's forgiveness of faults [wh]ich had he been awkward & inelegant would [ha]ve appeared very serious; to them, even more [tha]n to his person or his fortune, he owed the [reg]ard which almost every one was disposed [to] feel for him, and which Young Women in [pa]rticular were ~~disposed to feel~~ inclined to entertain. Their influ: [en]ce was acknowledged on the present occasion [by] Kitty, whose Anger they entirely dispelled; [an]d whose Chearfulness they had power not only [to r]estore, but to raise —. The Evening passed off [as] agreably as the one that had preceded it; they [con]tinued talking to each other, during the chief part [of] it, and such was the power of his Address, & the

Brilliancy of his Eyes, that when they par
for the Night, tho' Catherine had but a few h
before totally given up the idea, yet she fe
almost convinced again that he was really in
with her. She reflected on their past Convers
and tho' it had been on various & indifferen
subjects, and she could not exactly recollect
Speech on his side expressive of such a parti
she was still however nearly certain of it's
:ing so; But fearful of being vain enough to
:pose such a thing without sufficient reas
she resolved to suspend her final determin
:tion on it, till the next day, and more espec
till their parting which she thought wou
infallibly explain his regard if any he ha
The more she had seen of him, the more in
:ed was she to like him, & the more desir
that he should like *her*. She was convinced
his being naturally very clever and very wel

isposed, and that his thoughtlessness & negligen
ich tho' they appeared to *her* as very becoming
*him*, she was aware would by many people
considered as defects in his Character, merely
oceeded from a vivacity always pleasing in
ng Men, & were far from testifying a weak
vacant Understanding. Having settled this poi
thin herself, and being perfectly convinced by
own arguments of it's truth, she went to bed
high Spirits, determined to study his Charact
d watch his Behaviour still more the next
. She got up with the same good resolutions
d would probably have put them in execu:
n, had not ~~Nanny~~ Anne informed her as soon as
entered the room that Mr Edward Stanley
s already gone. At first she refused to credit
information, but when her Maid assured
that he had ordered a Carriage the evening
fore to be there at seven o'clock in the Morning
d that she herself had actually seen him depar

in it a little after eight, she could no longer [...]
:ny her belief to it. "And this, thought she t[...]
herself blushing with anger at her own foll[y]
this is the affection for me of which I was [...]
certain. Oh! what a silly Thing is Woma[n]
How vain, how unreasonable! To suppose th[at]
a young Man would be seriously attached in [the]
course of four & twenty hours, to a Girl who [has]
nothing to recommend her but a good pair of
eyes! And he is really gone! Gone perhaps [with-]
:out bestowing a thought on me! Oh! why
was not I up by eight o'clock? But it i[s a]
proper punishment for my Lazyness & Fo[lly]
and I am heartily glad of it. I deserve it all
ten times more for such insufferable va[nity.]
It will at least be of service to me in tha[t]
respect; it will teach me in future *not* to thi[nk]
Every Body is in love with me. Yet I *should* li[ke]
to have seen him before he went, for perhap[s]
it may be many Years before we meet ag[ain]

his Manner of leaving us however, he seems
have been perfectly indifferent about it. How
odd, that he should go without giving us
tice of it, or taking leave of any one! But
is just like a young Man, governed by the
him of the moment, or actuated merely by
love of doing anything oddly! Unaccount-
le Beings indeed! And young Women are
ually ridiculous! I shall soon begin to
ink like my Aunt that everything is
ing to sixes & sevens, and that the whole
ce of Mankind are degenerating." She was
st dressed, and on the point of leaving her
m to make her personal enquiries after
s Peterson, when Miss Stanley knocked at
r door, & on her being admitted began in
r usual strain a long harangue upon her
ther's being so shocking as to make Edward
at all, and upon Edward's being so horrid
to leave them at such an hour in the morn-
ig. "You have no idea, said she, how surprised

I was, when he came into my Room to bid me good bye —"

"Have you seen him then, this Morning?" said Kitty.

"Oh Yes! And I was so sleepy that I couldn't ... my eyes. And so he said, Camilla, goodbye to ... for I am going away. I have not time to take leave of any body else, and I dare not ... myself to see Kitty, for then you know I shall never get away—"

"Nonsense, said Kitty; he did not say that, ... he was in joke if he did."

"Oh! no I assure you he was as much ... earnest as he ever was in his life; he ... too much out of spirits to joke then. And he desired me when we all met at Breakfa... to give his Compts to your Aunt, and his lo... to you, for you was a nice Girl he said, ... he only wished it were in his power to ... more with you. You were just the Girl ... suit him, because you were so lively and goo...

-atured, and he wished with all his heart
-at you might not be married before he came
-ck, for there was nothing he liked better
-an being here. Oh! you have no idea what
-e things he said about you, till at last
-ell asleep and he went away. But he cer-
-inly is in love with you - I am sure he is.
-have thought so a great while I assure you."
-ow can you be so ridiculous?" said Kitty
-iling with pleasure; "I do not believe him
-be so easily affected. But he did desire
-s Love to me then? And wished I might
-t be married before his return? And said
-was a nice Girl, did he?"
-h! dear, yes, and I assure you it is the great-
-t praise in his opinion, that he can be-
-tow on any body; I can hardly ever persuade
-im to call me one, tho' I beg him some-
-mes for an hour together."
-nd do you really think that he was sorry
-go?"

"Oh! You can have no idea how wretched it m[akes]
him. He would not have gone this Month, if [my]
Father had not insisted on it; Edward told [me]
so himself yesterday. He said that he wis[hed]
with all his heart he had never promis[ed to]
go abroad, for that he repented it more a[nd]
more every day; that it interfered with a[ll]
his other schemes, and that since Papa [had]
spoke to him about it, he was more unw[ill-]
ing to leave Chetwynde than ever."

"Did he really say all this? And why w[ould]
your father insist upon his going?" "His leaving
England interfered with all his other plans, an[d]
his Conversation with Mr Stanley had made h[im]
still more averse to it." What can this Mea[n?]
"Why that he is excessively in love with [you,]
to be sure; what other plans can he hav[e?]
And I suppose my father said that if he [had]
not been going abroad, he should have w[ished]
him to marry you immediately. — But I mu[st]

and see your Aunt's plants— There is one of
em that I quite doat on— and two or three
ore besides—"
Can Camilla's explanation be true? said
therine to herself, when her freind had
ft the room. And after all my doubts and
certainties, can Stanley really be averse to
aving England for my *sake* only? "His
ans interrupted." And what indeed can
s plans be, but towards Marriage? Yet
*soon* to be in love with me!— But it is
effect perhaps only of a warmth of
rt which to *me* is the highest recom:
ndation in any one. A Heart disposed
love— And such under the appearance
so much Gaity and Inattention, is Stanly's!
! how much does it endear him to me!
t he is gone— Gone perhaps for Years—
liged to tear himself from what he most
es, his happiness is sacrificed to the vani:
of his Father! In what anguish he must

have left the house! Unable to see me, or
bid me adieu, while I, senseless wretch, w
daring to sleep. This, then explains his lea
us at such a time of day—. He could not b
himself to see me—. Charming Young Ma
How much must you have suffered! I
that it was impossible for one so elegan
and so well bred, to leave any Family i
such a Manner, but for a Motive like t
unanswerable." Satisfied, beyond the po
of Change, of this, she went in high sp
:irits to her Aunt's apartment, withou
giving a Moment's recollection on the
:nity of Young Women, or the unaccou
:ble conduct of Young Men. ——————

Kitty continued in this state of satisfaction
during the remainder of the Stanley's visi
Who took their leave with many pressing
invitations to visit them in London, when
as Camilla said, she might have an

opportunity of becoming acquainted with that sweet girl Augusta Halifax— Rather (thought Kitty,) of seeing my d^r Mary Wynne again— Mrs ~~Peterson~~ Percival in answer to Mrs Stanley's invitation replied— That she looked upon London as the hot house of Vice where virtue had long been banished from Society & wickedness of every description was daily gaining ground— that Kitty was of herself sufficiently inclined to give way to, & indulge in vicious inclinations— & therefore was the last girl in the world to be trusted in London, as she would be totally unable to withstand temptation—

After the departure of the Stanleys Kitty returned to her usual occupations, but Alas! they had lost their power of pleasing. Her bower alone retained its interest in her feelings, & perhaps that was owing to the particular remembrance it brought to her mind of Edw^d Stanley.

The Summer passed away unmarked by any incident worth narrating, ~~or any~~ pleasure to Catharine save one, which arose from the receipt of a letter from her friend Cecilia now Mrs Lascelles announcing the speedy return of herself & Husband to England. A correspondance productive indeed of little pleasure to either party had been established between Camilla & Catharine. The latter had now lost the only satisfaction she had ever received from the letters of Miss Stanley, as that young Lady having informed her Friend of the departure of her Brother to Lyons now never mentioned his name — Her letters seldom contained any Intelligence except ~~the account~~ a description of some new Article of Dress, an enumeration of various engagements, a panegyric on Augustus Halifax & perhaps a little abuse of the unfortunate Sir Peter —

The Grove, for so was the Mansion of Mrs Percival
at Chetwynde denominated was situated within
ve miles from ~~the town~~ Exeter, but though
at Lady possessed a carriage & horses of her
own, it was seldom that Catharine could
revail on her to visit that town for the
urpose of shopping, on account of the
any Officers perpetually Quartered there
infested the principal Streets—A company
strolling players in their way from some
Neighbouring Races having opened a
mporary Theatre there—Mrs Percival was
revailed on by her Niece to indulge
r by attending the performance ~~there~~
ce during their stay—Mrs Percival
sisted on paying Miss Dudley the compliment
inviting her to join the party, when a new
ifficulty arose, from the necessity of having
to attend them
me Gentleman ~~of their party~~ —

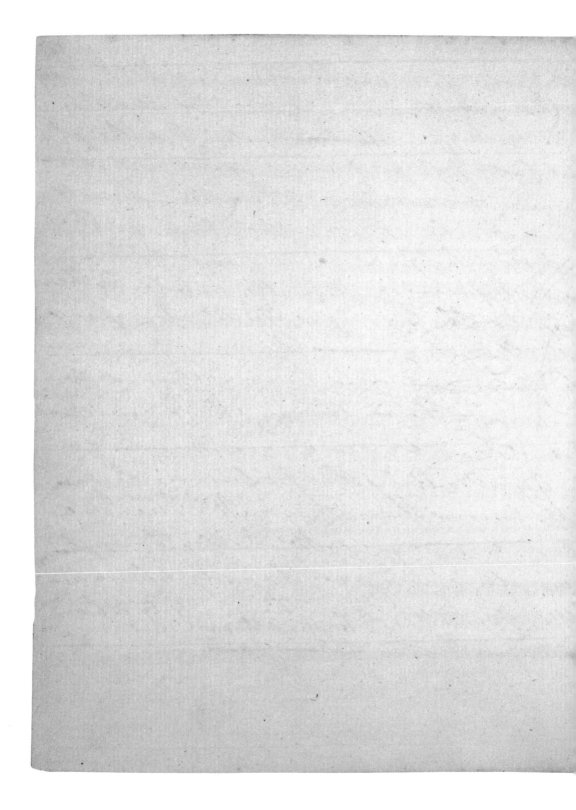

on re entering his circular domain, his round-Robin of perpetual peace; where enjoyment had no end, and calamity no commencement, his spirits became wonderfully composed, and a delicious calm extended itself through every nerve – With his pocket handkerchief (once hemmed by the genius of the too susceptible Rosa) he wiped the morbid moisture from his brow; then flew to the Boudoir of his Maria – And, did she not fly to meet her Frederick? Did she not dart from the couch on which she had so gracefully reclined, and bounding like an agile fawn over the intervening foot stool, precipitate herself into his arms? Does she not, though fainting between every syllable, breathe forth as it were by installments her Frederick's adored name? Who is there of perception so obtuse as not to realize the touching scene? Who, of ear so dull as not to catch the soft murmurs of

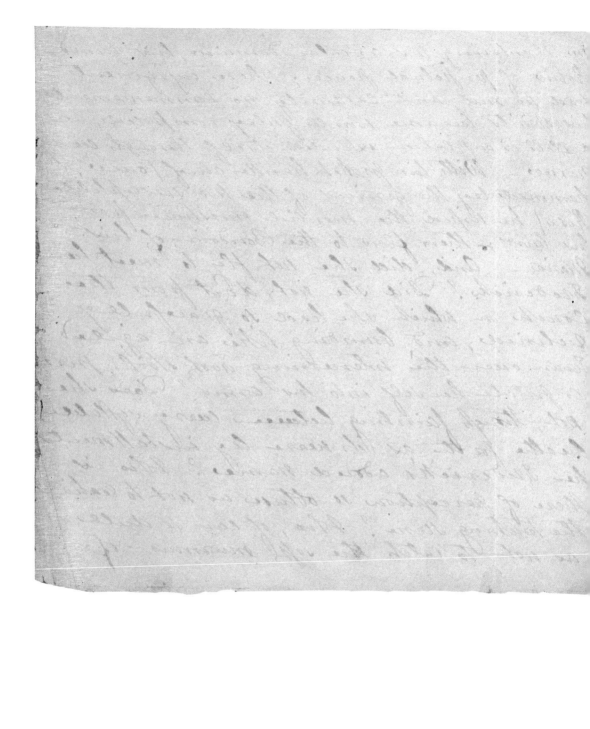

Maria's voice! Ah! Who? The heart of every
sympathetic reader repeats, Ah, Who?
vain Echo! Vain sympathy! There is
no meeting – no murmur – no Maria –
It is not in the ~~language~~ power of
language however potent; nor in that
of style, however diffuse to render justice
to the astonishment of Mr. Gower –
arming himself with a mahogany ruler
which some fatality had placed on Maria's
writing table, ~~and~~ calling repeatedly on
her beloved name, he rushed forward
to examine the adjacent apartments –
In the Dressing room of his lost one he
had the melancholy satisfaction of picking
up a curl paper, and a gust of wind,
as he re entered the Boudoir, swept from
the table & placed at his feet a skein
of black sewing silk, – These were the
only traces of Maria!! Carefully locking
the doors of these now desolate rooms,
burying the key deep in his waistcoat
pocket, & the mystery of Maria's disappearance yet deeper in his heart
of hearts. Mr. Gower left his once happy

ome and sought a supper, and a Bed, n the house of the hospitable Mrs Willis — There was an oppression n his chest which made him extremely uncomfortable; he regretted that instead of the skein of silk carefully wrapped up in the curl paper & placed beneath his pillow he had not rather swallowed Laudanum — it would have been, in all probability more efficacious — At last, Mr Gordon slept a troubled sleep, and in due course of time he dreamt a troubled dream — He dreamed of Marie, as how could he less? She stood by his Bed side, in her sleeping gown — one hand held an open book, with the forefinger of the other she pointed to this ominous passage — "Tantôt c'est un vide; tantôt c'est un poids qui nous ennuie; tantôt c'est un poids qui nous oppresse" — The unfortunate Frederick uttered a deep groan — & as the vision closed the volume he observed these characters strangely imprinted on the cover — Rolandi — Berners Street

Who was this ~~dangerous~~ dangerous Rolandi? Doubtless a Bravo or a Monk — possibly both — and what was he to Maria? Vainly he would have dared the worst, and put the fatal question — the semblance of Maria raised her monitory finger, and interdicted speech — yet, some words she spoke, or seemed to speak herself; Mr. Gower could distinguish only these — Search — Cupboard — Top shelf — Once more he essayed to speak, but it was all bewilderment — He heard strange Demon-like sounds; hissing and spitting — he smelt an unearthly smell — the agony became unbearable, and he awoke — Maria had vanished; the Rush light was expiring in the Socket; and the benevolent Mrs. Wilkis entering his room, threw open the Shutters, and in accordance with her own warmth of heart admitted the full blaze of a Summer morning's Sun —

JHL

But what found he on reentering
that ~~garden~~ circle of peace, that round Abo
of perpetual peace

# VOLUME THE THIRD

*Jane Austen—May 6th 1792.*

## CONTENTS



To Miss Mary Lloyd,
The following Novel is by permission
Dedicated,
by her Obedt humble Servt

THE AUTHOR

## *Evelyn*

IN a retired part of the County of Sussex there is a village (for what I know to the Contrary) called Evelyn, perhaps one of the most beautiful Spots in the south of England. A Gentleman passing through it on horseback about twenty years ago, was so entirely of my opinion in this respect, that he put up at the little Alehouse in it & enquired with great earnestness whether there were any house to be lett in the Parish. The Landlady, who as well as every one else in Evelyn was remarkably amiable, shook her head at this question, but seemed unwilling to give him any answer. He could not bear this uncertainty—yet knew not how to obtain the information he desired. To repeat a question which had already appear'd to make the good woman uneasy was impossible—. He turned from her in visible agitation. "What a situation am I in!" said he to himself as he walked to the window and threw up the sash. He found himself revived by the Air, which he felt to a much greater degree when he had opened the window than he had done before. Yet it was but for a moment—. The agonizing pain[1] of Doubt & Suspence again weighed down his Spirits. The good woman who had watched in eager silence every turn of his Countenance with that benevolence which characterizes the inhabitants of Evelyn, intreated him to tell her the cause of his uneasiness. "Is there anything Sir in my power to do that may releive your Greifs—Tell me in what manner I can sooth them, & beleive me that the freindly balm of Comfort and Assistance shall not be wanting; for indeed Sir I have a simpathetic Soul."

"Amiable Woman (said Mr Gower, affected almost to tears by this generous offer) This Greatness of mind in one to whom I am almost a Stranger, serves but to make me the more warmly wish for a house in this sweet village—. What would I not give to be your Neighbour, to be blessed with your Acquaintance, and with the farther knowledge of your virtues! Oh! with what pleasure would I form myself by such an example! Tell me then, best of Women, is there no possibility?—I cannot speak—You know my meaning——."

"Alas! Sir, replied Mrs Willis, there is *none*. Every house in this village, from the sweetness of the Situation, & the purity of the Air, in which neither Misery, Illhealth, or Vice are ever wafted, is inhabited. And yet, (after a short pause) there is a Family, who tho' warmly attached to the spot, yet from a peculiar Generosity of Disposition would perhaps be willing to oblige you with[2] their house." He eagerly caught at this idea, and having gained a direction to the place,[3] he set off immediately on his walk to it. As he approached the House, he was delighted with its situation. It was in the exact centre of a small circular paddock, which was enclosed by a regular paling, & bordered with a plantation of Lombardy poplars, & Spruce firs alternatively placed in three rows. A gravel walk ran through this beautiful Shrubbery, and as the remainder of the paddock was unincumbered with any other Timber, the surface of it perfectly even & smooth, and grazed by four white Cows which were disposed at equal distances from each other, the whole appearance of the place as Mr Gower entered the Paddock was uncommonly striking. A beautifully-rounded, gravel road without any turn or interruption led immediately to the house. Mr Gower rang—the Door was soon opened. "Are Mr & Mrs Webb at home?" "My Good Sir they are"—replied the Servant; And leading the way, conducted Mr Gower upstairs into a very elegant Dressing room, where a Lady rising from her seat, welcomed him with all the Generosity which Mrs Willis had attributed to the Family.

"Welcome best of Men—Welcome to this House, & to everything it contains. William, tell your Master of the happiness I enjoy—invite him to partake of it—. Bring up some Chocolate immediately; Spread a Cloth in the dining Parlour, and carry in

---

1 idea *erased.*

2 the remainder of *erased.*

3 House *erased.*

the venison pasty—. In the mean time let the Gentleman have some sandwiches, and bring in a Basket of Fruit—Send up some Ices and a bason of Soup, and do not forget some Jellies and Cakes." Then turning to Mr Gower, & taking out her purse, "Accept this my good Sir,—. Beleive me you are welcome to everything that is in my power to bestow.—I wish my purse were weightier, but Mr Webb must make up my deficiencies—. I know he has cash in the house to the amount of an hundred pounds, which he shall bring you immediately." Mr Gower felt overpowered by her generosity as he put the purse in his pocket, and from the excess[4] of his Gratitude, could scarcely express himself intelligibly when he accepted her offer of the hundred pounds. Mr Webb soon entered the room, and repeated every protestation of Freindship & Cordiality which his Lady had already made.[5] The Chocolate, The Sandwiches, the Jellies, the Cakes, the Ice, and the Soup soon made their appearance, and Mr Gower having tasted something of all, and pocketted the rest, was conducted into the dining parlour, where he eat a most excellent Dinner & partook of the most exquisite Wines, while Mr and Mrs Webb stood by him still pressing him to eat and drink a little more. "And now my good Sir, said Mr Webb, when Mr Gower's repast was concluded, what else can we do to contribute to your happiness and express the Affection we bear you.[6] Tell us what you wish more to receive, and depend upon our gratitude for the communication of your wishes." "Give me then your house & Grounds; I ask for nothing else." "It is yours, exclaimed both at once; from this moment it is yours." The Agreement concluded on and the present accepted by Mr Gower, Mr Webb rang to have the Carriage ordered, telling William at the same time to call the Young Ladies.

"Best of Men, said Mrs Webb, we will not long intrude upon your Time."

"Make no Apologies dear Madam, replied Mr Gower, You are welcome to stay this half hour if you like it."

They both burst forth into raptures of Admiration at his politeness, which they agreed served only to make their Conduct appear more inexcusable in trespassing on his time.

The Young Ladies soon entered the room. The eldest of them was about seventeen, the other, several years younger. Mr Gower had no sooner fixed his Eyes on Miss Webb than he felt that something more was necessary to his happiness than the house he had just received—Mrs Webb introduced him to her daughter. "Our dear freind Mr Gower my Love—He has been so good as to accept of this house, small as it is, & to promise to keep it for ever." "Give me leave to assure you Sir, said Miss Webb, that I am highly sensible of your kindness in this respect, which from the shortness of my Father's & Mother's acquaintance with you, is more than usually flattering."

Mr Gower bowed—"You are too obliging Ma'am—I assure you that I like the house

4 effusions *erased.*

5 before expressed *erased.*

6 for *erased before* you.

extremely—and if they would complete their generosity by giving me their elder daughter in marriage with a handsome portion, I should have nothing more to wish for." This compliment brought a blush into the cheeks of the lovely Miss Webb, who seemed however to refer herself to her father & Mother. *They* looked delighted at each other—At length Mrs Webb breaking silence, said—"We bend under a weight of obligations to you which we can never repay. Take our girl, take our Maria, and on her must the difficult task fall, of endeavouring to make some return to so much Benefiscence." Mr Webb added, "Her fortune is but ten thousand pounds, which is almost too small a sum to be offered." This objection however being instantly removed by the generosity of Mr Gower, who declared himself satisfied with the sum mentioned, Mr & Mrs Webb, with their youngest daughter took their leave, and on the next day, the nuptials of their eldest with Mr Gower were celebrated.—This amiable Man now found himself perfectly happy; united to a very lovely and deserving young woman, with an handsome fortune, an elegant house, settled in the village of Evelyn, & by that means enabled to cultivate his acquaintance with Mrs Willis, could he have a wish ungratified?—For some months he found that he could *not,* till one day as he was walking in the Shrubbery with Maria leaning on his arm, they observed a rose full-blown lying on the gravel; it had fallen from a rose tree which with three others had been planted by Mr Webb to give a pleasing variety to the walk. These four Rose trees served also to mark the quarters of the Shrubbery, by which means the Traveller might always know how far in his progress round the Paddock he was got—. Maria stooped to pick up the beautiful flower, and with all her Family Generosity presented it to her Husband. "My dear Frederic, said she, pray take this charming rose." "Rose! exclaimed Mr Gower—. Oh! Maria, of what does not that remind me! Alas my poor Sister, how have I neglected you!" The truth was that Mr Gower was the only son of a very large Family, of which Miss Rose Gower was the thirteenth daughter. This Young Lady whose merits deserved a better fate than she met with, was the darling of her relations—From the clearness of her skin & the Brilliancy of her Eyes, she was fully entitled to all their partial affection. Another circumstance contributed to the general Love they bore her, and that was one of the finest heads of hair in the world. A few Months before her Brother's marriage, her heart had been engaged by the attentions and charms of a young Man whose high rank and expectations seemed to foretell objections from his Family to a match which would be highly desirable to theirs. Proposals were made on the young Man's part, and proper objections on his Father's—He was desired to return from Carlisle where he was with his beloved Rose, to the family seat in Sussex. He was obliged to comply, and the angry father then finding from his Conversation how determined he was to marry no other woman, sent him for a fortnight to the Isle of Wight under the care of the Family Chaplain, with the hope of overcoming his Constancy by Time and Absence in a foreign Country. They accordingly prepared to bid a long adieu to England—The young Nobleman was not allowed to see his Rosa. They set sail—A storm arose which baffled the arts of the Seamen. The Vessel was wrecked on the coast of Calshot and every Soul on board perished. The sad Event soon reached Carlisle, and the beautiful Rose was affected by it, beyond the power of Expression. It was to soften her affliction by obtaining a picture of her unfortunate Lover that her brother undertook a Journey into Sussex, where he hoped that his petition would not be rejected, by the severe yet afflicted Father. When he reached Evelyn he was not many miles from —— Castle, but the pleasing events which befell him in that place had for a while made him totally forget the object of his Journey & his unhappy Sister. The little incident of the rose however brought everything concerning her to his recollection again, & he bitterly repented his neglect. He returned to the house immediately and agitated by[7] Greif, Apprehension and Shame wrote the following Letter to Rosa.

July 14th—. Evelyn

My dearest Sister

As it is now four months since I left Carlisle, during which period I have not once written to you, You will perhaps unjustly accuse me of Neglect and Forgetfulness. Alas! I blush when I own the truth of your Accusation.—Yet if you are still alive, do not think too harshly of me, or suppose that I could for a moment forget the situation of my Rose. Beleive me I will forget you no longer, but will hasten as soon as possible to —— Castle if I find by your answer that you are still alive. Maria joins me in every dutiful and affectionate wish, & I am yours sincerely

F. Gower.

He waited in the most anxious expectation for an answer to his Letter, which arrived as soon as the great distance from Carlisle would admit of.—But alas, it came not from[8] Rosa.

Carlisle July 17th

Dear Brother

My Mother has taken the liberty of opening your Letter to poor Rose, as she has been dead these six weeks. Your long absence and continued Silence gave us all great uneasiness and hastened her to the Grave. Your Journey to —— Castle therefore may be spared. You do not tell us where you have been since the time of your quitting Carlisle, nor in any way account for your tedious absence, which gives us some surprise. We all unite in Compts to Maria, & beg to know who she is—.

Yr affec:te Sister
M. Gower.

---

7 with *erased.*

8 for *erased.*

This Letter, by which Mr Gower was obliged to attribute to his own conduct, his Sister's death, was so violent a shock to his feelings, that in spite of his living at Evelyn where Illness was scarcely ever heard of, he was attacked by a fit of the gout, which confining him to his own room afforded an opportunity to Maria of shining in that favourite character of Sir Charles Grandison's, a nurse. No woman could ever appear more amiable than Maria did under such circumstances, and at last by her unremitting attentions had the pleasure of seeing him gradually recover the use of his feet. It was a blessing by no means lost on him, for he was no sooner in a condition to leave the house, than he mounted his horse, and rode to —— Castle, wishing to find whether his Lordship softened by his Son's death, might have been brought to consent to the match, had both he and Rosa been alive. His amiable Maria followed him with her Eyes till she could see him no longer, and then sinking into her chair overwhelmed with Greif, found that in his absence she could enjoy no comfort.

Mr Gower arrived late in the evening at the castle, which was situated on a woody Eminence commanding a beautiful prospect of the Sea. Mr Gower did not dislike the situation, tho' it was certainly greatly inferior[9] to that of his own house. There was an irregularity in the fall of the ground, and a profusion of old Timber which appeared to him illsuited to the stile of the Castle, for it being a building of a very ancient[10] date, he thought it required the Paddock of Evelyn lodge to form a Contrast, and enliven the structure. The gloomy appearance of the old Castle frowning on him as he followed its' winding approach, struck him with terror. Nor did he think himself safe, till he was introduced into the Drawing room where the Family were assembled to tea. Mr Gower was a perfect stranger to every one in the Circle but tho' he was always timid in the Dark and easily terrified when alone, he did not want that more necessary and more noble courage which enabled him without a Blush to enter a large party of superior Rank, whom he had never seen before, & to take his Seat amongst them with perfect Indifference. The name of Gower was not unknown to Lord ——. He felt distressed & astonished; yet rose and received him with all the politeness of a well-bred Man. Lady —— who felt a deeper sorrow at the loss of her Son, than his Lordships harder heart was capable of, could hardly keep her Seat when she found that he was the Brother of her lamented Henry's[11] Rosa. "My Lord said Mr Gower as soon as he was seated, You are perhaps surprised at receiving a visit from a Man whom you could not have the least expectation of seeing here. But my Sister my unfortunate Sister is the real cause of my thus troubling you: That luckless Girl is now no more—and tho' *she* can receive no pleasure from the intelligence, yet for the satisfaction of her Family I wish to know whether the Death of this unhappy Pair has made an impression on your heart sufficiently strong to obtain that consent to their Marriage which in

9 superior *erased.*

10 old *erased.*

11 *Erasure illegible.*

happier circumstances you would not be persuaded to give supposing that they now were both alive." His Lordship seemed lossed in astonishment. Lady ——— could not support the mention of her son, and left the room in tears; the rest of the Family remained attentively listening, almost persuaded that Mr Gower was distracted. "Mr Gower, replied his Lordship This is a very odd question—It appears to me that you are supposing an impossibility—No one can more sincerely regret the death of my Son than I have always done, and it gives me great concern to know that Miss Gower's was hastened by his—. Yet to suppose them alive is destroying at once the Motive for a change in my sentiments concerning the affair." "My Lord, replied Mr Gower in anger, I see that you are a most inflexible Man, and that not even the death of your Son can make you wish his future Life happy. I will no longer detain your Lordship. I see, I plainly see that you are a very vile Man—And now I have the honour of wishing all your Lordships, and Ladyships a good Night." He immediately left the room, forgetting in the heat of his Anger the lateness of the hour, which at any other time would have made him tremble, & leaving the whole Company unanimous in their opinion of his being Mad. When however he had mounted his horse and the great Gates of the Castle had shut him out, he felt an universal tremor through out his whole frame. If we consider his Situation indeed, alone, on horseback, as late in the year as August, and in the day, as nine o'clock, with no light to direct him but that of the Moon almost full, and the Stars which alarmed him by their twinkling, who can refrain from pitying him?—No house within a quarter of a mile, and a Gloomy Castle blackened by the deep shade of Walnuts and Pines, behind him.—He felt indeed almost distracted with his fears, and shutting his Eyes till he arrived at the Village to prevent his seeing either Gipsies or Ghosts, he rode on a full gallop all the way. On his return home, he rang the house-bell, but no one appeared, a second time he rang, but the door was not opened, a third & a fourth with as little success, when observing the dining parlour window open he leapt in, & persued his way through the house till he reached Maria's Dressingroom, where he found all the servants assembled at tea. Surprized at so very unusual a sight, he fainted, on his recovery he found himself on the Sofa, with his wife's maid kneeling by him, chafing his temples with Hungary water—. From her he learned that his beloved Maria had been so much grieved at his departure that she died of a broken heart about 3 hours after his departure.

He then became sufficiently composed to give necessary orders for her funeral which took place the Monday following this being the Saturday—When Mr Gower had settled the order of the procession he set out himself to Carlisle, to give vent to his sorrow in the bosom of his family—He arrived there in high health & spirits, after a delightful journey of 3 days & a 1/2—What was his surprize on entering the Breakfast parlour to see Rosa his beloved Rosa seated on a Sofa; at the sight of him she fainted & would have fallen had not a Gentleman sitting with his back to the door, started up & saved her from sinking to the ground—She very soon came to herself & then introduced this gentleman to her Brother as her Husband a Mr Davenport—

But my dearest Rosa said the astonished Gower, I thought you were dead & buried. Why my dr Frederick replied Rosa I wished you to think so, hoping that you would spread the report about the country & it would thus by some means reach —— Castle—By this I hoped some how or other to touch the hearts of its inhabitants. It was not till the day before yesterday that I heard of the death of my beloved Henry which I learned from Mr D—— who concluded by offering me his hand. I accepted it with transport, & was married yesterday—Mr Gower, embraced his sister & shook hands with Mr Davenport, he then took a stroll into the town—As he passed by a public house he called for a pot of beer, which was brought him immediately by his old friend Mrs Willis—

Great was his astonishment at seeing Mrs Willis in Carlisle. But not forgetful of the respect he owed her, he dropped on one knee, & received the frothy cup from her, more grateful to him than Nectar—He instantly made her an offer of his hand & heart, which she graciously condescended to accept, telling him that she was only on a visit to her cousin, who kept the *Anchor* & should be ready to return to Evelyn, whenever he chose—The next morning they were married & immediately proceeded to Evelyn—When he reached home, he recollected that he had never written to Mr & Mrs Webb to inform them of the death of their daughter, which he rightly supposed they knew nothing of, as they never took in any newspapers—He immediately dispatched the following Letter—

Evelyn—Augst 19th 1809—

Dearest Madam,

How can words express the poignancy of my feelings! Our Maria, our beloved Maria is no more, she breathed her last, on Saturday the 12th of Augst—I see you now in an agony of grief lamenting not your own, but my loss—Rest satisfied I am happy, possessed of my lovely Sarah what more can I wish for?—

I remain
respectfully Yours

F. Gower

Westgate Builgs Augst 22d

Generous, best of Men

how truly we rejoice to hear of your present welfare & happiness! & how truly grateful are we for your unexampled generosity in writing to condole with us on the late unlucky accident which befel our Maria—I have enclosed a draught on our banker for 30 pounds, which Mr Webb joins with me in entreating you & the aimiable Sarah to accept—

Your most grateful
Anne Augusta Webb

Mr & Mrs Gower resided many years at Evelyn enjoying perfect happiness the just reward of their virtues. The only alteration which took place at Evelyn was that Mr & Mrs Davenport settled there in Mrs Willis's former abode & were for many years the proprietors of the White Horse Inn—

# *Catharine*

## OR THE BOWER

### *To Miss Austen*

MADAM

Encouraged by your warm patronage of The beautiful Cassandra, and The History of England, which through your generous support, have obtained a place in every library in the Kingdom, and run through threescore Editions, I take the liberty of begging the same Exertions in favour of the following Novel, which I humbly flatter myself, possesses Merit beyond any already published, or any that will ever in future appear, except such as may proceed from the pen of Your Most Grateful Humble Servt

THE AUTHOR

Steventon August 1792—

---

CATHARINE[12] had the misfortune, as many heroines have had before her, of losing her Parents when she was very young, and of being brought up under the care of a Maiden Aunt, who while she tenderly loved her, watched over her conduct with so scrutinizing a severity, as to make it very doubtful to many people, and to Catharine[1] amongst the rest, whether she loved her or not. She had frequently been deprived of a real pleasure through this jealous Caution, had been sometimes obliged to relinquish a Ball because an Officer was to be there, or to dance with a Partner of her Aunt's introduction in preference to one of her own Choice. But her Spirits were naturally good, and not easily depressed, and she possessed such a fund of vivacity and good humour as could only be damped by some serious vexation.—Besides these antidotes against every disappointment, and consolations under them, she had another, which afforded her constant releif in all her misfortunes, and that was a fine shady Bower, the work of her own infantine Labours assisted by those of two young Companions who had

[12] Kitty, *erased here, stands elsewhere.*

resided in the same village—. To this Bower, which terminated a very pleasant and retired walk in her Aunt's Garden, she always wandered whenever anything disturbed her, and it possessed such a charm over her senses, as constantly to tranquillize her mind & quiet her spirits—Solitude & reflection might perhaps have had the same effect in her Bed Chamber, yet Habit had so strengthened the idea which Fancy had first suggested, that such a thought never occurred to Kitty who was firmly persuaded that her Bower alone could restore her to herself. Her imagination was warm, and in her Freindships, as well as in the whole tenure of her Mind, she was enthousiastic. This beloved Bower had been the united work of herself and two amiable Girls, for whom since her earliest Years, she had felt the tenderest regard. They were the daughters of the Clergyman of the Parish with whose Family, while it had continued there, her Aunt had been on the most intimate terms, and the little Girls tho' separated for the greatest part of the Year by the different Modes of their Education, were constantly together during the holidays of the Miss Wynnes; [they were companions in their walks, their Schemes & Amusements, and while the sweetness of their dispositions had prevented any serious Quarrels, the trifling disputes which it was impossible wholly to avoid, had been far from lessening their affection].[13] In those days of happy Childhood, now so often regretted by Kitty this arbour had been formed, and separated perhaps for ever from these dear freinds, it encouraged more than any other place the tender and Melancholy recollections of hours rendered pleasant by *them,* at one [*sic*] so sorrowful, yet so soothing! It was now two years since the death of Mr Wynne, and the consequent dispersion of his Family who had been left by it in great distress. They had been reduced to a state of absolute dependance on some relations, who though very opulent and very nearly connected with them, had with difficulty been prevailed on to contribute anything towards their Support. Mrs Wynne was fortunately spared the knowledge & participation of their distress, by her release from a painful illness a few months before the death of her husband.—The eldest daughter had been obliged to accept the offer of one of her cousins to equip her for the East Indies, and tho' infinitely against her inclinations had been necessitated to embrace the only possibility that was offered to her, of a Maintenance; Yet it was *one,* so opposite to all her ideas of Propriety, so contrary to her Wishes, so repugnant to her feelings, that she would almost have preferred Servitude to it, had Choice been allowed her—. Her personal Attractions had gained her a husband as soon as she had arrived at Bengal, and she had now been married nearly a twelvemonth. Splendidly, yet unhappily married. United to a Man of double her own age, whose disposition was not amiable, and whose Manners were unpleasing, though his Character was respectable. Kitty had heard twice from her freind since her marriage, but her Letters were always unsatisfactory, and though she did not openly avow her feelings, yet every line proved her to be Unhappy. She spoke with pleasure of nothing, but of those

[13] *Erased.*

Amusements which they had shared together and which could return no more, and seemed to have no happiness in veiw but that of returning to England again. Her sister had been taken by another relation the Dowager Lady Halifax as a companion to her Daughters, and had accompanied her family into Scotland about the same time of Cecilia's leaving England. From Mary therefore Kitty had the power of hearing more frequently, but her Letters were scarcely more comfortable—. There was not indeed that hopelessness of sorrow in her situation as in her sisters; she was not married, and could yet look forward to a change in her circumstances, but situated for the present without any immediate hope of it, in a family where, tho' all were her relations she had no freind, she wrote usually in depressed Spirits, which her separation from her Sister and her Sister's Marriage had greatly contributed to make so.— Divided thus from the two she loved best on Earth, while Cecilia & Mary were still more endeared to her by their loss, everything that brought a remembrance of them was doubly cherished, & the Shrubs they had planted, & the keepsakes they had given were rendered sacred—. The living of Chetwynde was now in the possession of a Mr Dudley, whose Family unlike the Wynnes were productive only of vexation & trouble to Mrs Percival[14] and her Neice. Mr Dudley, who was the Younger Son of a very noble Family, of a Family more famed for their Pride than their opulence, tenacious of his Dignity, and jealous of his rights, was forever quarrelling, if not with Mrs P. herself, with her Steward and Tenants concerning tythes, and with the principal Neighbours themselves concerning the respect & parade, he exacted. His Wife, an ill-educated, untaught woman of ancient family, was proud of that family almost without knowing why, and like him too was haughty and quarrelsome, without considering for what. Their only daughter, who inherited the ignorance, the insolence, & pride of her parents, was from that Beauty of which she was unreasonably vain, considered by them as an irresistable Creature, and looked up to as the future restorer, by a Splendid Marriage, of the dignity which their reduced Situation and Mr Dudley's being obliged to take orders for a Country Living had so much lessened. They at once despised the Percivals as people of mean family, and envied them as people of fortune. They were jealous of their being more respected than themselves and while they affected to consider them as of no Consequence, were continually seeking to lessen them in the opinion of the Neighbourhood by Scandalous & Malicious reports. Such a family as this, was ill-calculated to console Kitty for the loss of the Wynnes, or to fill up by their Society, those occasionally irksome hours which in so retired a Situation would sometimes occur for want of a Companion. Her aunt was most excessively fond of her, and miserable if she saw her for a moment out of spirits; Yet she lived in such constant apprehension of her marrying imprudently if she were allowed the opportunity of choosing, and was so dissatisfied with her behaviour when she saw her with Young Men, for it was, from her natural disposition remarkably open and unreserved, that

---

[14] *Substituted here and elsewhere for* Peterson.

though she frequently wished for her Neice's sake, that the Neighbourhood were larger, and that She had used herself to mix more with it, yet the recollection of there being young Men in almost every Family in it, always conquered the Wish. The same fears that prevented Mrs Peterson's joining much in the Society of her Neighbours, led her equally to avoid inviting her relations to spend any time in her House—She had therefore constantly regretted the annual attempt of a distant relation to visit her at Chetwynde, as there was a young Man in the Family of whom she had heard many traits that alarmed her. This Son was however now on his travels, and the repeated solicitations of Kitty, joined to a consciousness of having declined with too little Ceremony the frequent overtures of her Freinds to be admitted, and a real wish to see them herself, easily prevailed on her to press with great Earnestness the pleasure of a visit from them during the Summer. Mr & Mrs Stanley were accordingly to come, and Catharine, in having an object to look forward to, a something to expect that must inevitably releive the dullness of a constant tete a tete with her Aunt, was so delighted, and her spirits so elevated, that for the three or four days immediately preceding their Arrival, she could scarcely fix herself to any employment. In thispoint Mrs Percival always thought her defective, and frequently complained of a want of Steadiness & perseverance in her occupations, which were by no means congenial to the eagerness of Kitty's Disposition, and perhaps not often met with in any young person. The tediousness too of her Aunt's conversation and the want of agreable Companions greatly increased this desire of Change in her Employments, for Kitty found herself much sooner tired of Reading, Working, or Drawing, in Mrs Peterson's parlour than in her own Arbour, where Mrs Peterson for fear of its being damp never accompanied her.

As her Aunt prided herself on the exact propriety and Neatness with which everything in her Family was conducted, and had no higher Satisfaction than that of knowing her house to be always in complete Order, as her fortune was good, and her Establishment Ample, few were the preparations necessary for the reception of her Visitors. The day of their arrival so long expected, at length came, and the Noise of the Coach & 4 as it drove round the sweep, was to Catherine a more interesting sound, than the Music of an Italian Opera, which to most Heroines is the hight of Enjoyment. Mr and Mrs Stanley were people of Large Fortune & high Fashion. He was a Member of the house of Commons, and they were therefore most agreably necessitated to reside half the Year in Town; where Miss Stanley had been attended by the most capital Masters from the time of her being six years old to the last Spring, which comprehending a period of twelve Years had been dedicated to the acquirement of Accomplishments which were now to be displayed and in a few Years entirely neglected. She was not inelegant in her appearance, rather handsome, and naturally not deficient in Abilities; but those Years which ought to have been spent in the attainment of useful knowledge and Mental Improvement, had been all bestowed in learning Drawing, Italian and Music, more especially the latter, and she now united to these Accomplishments, an Understanding unimproved by reading and a Mind totally devoid either of Taste or Judgement. Her temper was by Nature good, but unassisted by reflection, she had neither patience under Disappointment, nor could sacrifice her own inclinations to promote the happiness of others. All her Ideas were towards the Elegance of her appearance, the fashion of her dress, and the Admiration she wished them to excite. She professed a love of Books without Reading, was Lively without Wit, and generally good humoured without Merit. Such was Camilla Stanley; and Catherine, who was prejudiced by her appearance, and who from her solitary Situation was ready to like anyone, tho' her Understanding and Judgement would not otherwise have been easily satisfied, felt almost convinced when she saw her, that Miss Stanley would be the very companion She wanted, and in some degree make amends for the loss of Cecilia & Mary Wynne. She therefore attached herself to Camilla from the first day of her arrival, and from being the only young People in the house, they were by inclination constant Companions. Kitty was herself a great reader, tho' perhaps not a very deep one, and felt therefore highly delighted to find that Miss Stanley was equally fond of it. Eager to know that their sentiments as to Books were similar, she very soon began questioning her new Acquaintance on the subject; but though She was well read in Modern history herself, she chose rather to speak first of Books of a lighter kind, of Books universally read and Admired, [and that have given rise perhaps to more frequent Arguments than any other of the same sort].[15]

"You have read Mrs Smith's Novels, I suppose?" said she to her Companion—. "Oh! Yes, replied the other, and I am quite delighted with them—They are the sweetest things in the world—" "And which do you prefer of them?" "Oh! dear, I think there is no comparison between them—Emmeline is *so much* better than any of the others—" "Many people think so, I know; but there does not appear so great a disproportion in their Merits to *me;* do you think it is better written?" "Oh! I do not know anything about *that*—but it is better in *everything*—Besides, Ethelinde is so long—" "That is a very common Objection I believe, said Kitty, but for my own part, if a book is well written, I always find it too short." "So do I, only I get tired of it before it is finished." "But did not you find the story of Ethelinde very interesting? And the Descriptions of Grasmere, are not the[y] Beautiful?" "Oh! I missed them all, because I was in such a hurry to know the end of it—Then from an easy transition she added, We are going to the Lakes this Autumn, and I am quite Mad with Joy; Sir Henry Devereux has promised to go with us, and that will make it so pleasant, you know—"

"I dare say it will; but I think it is a pity that Sir Henry's powers of pleasing were not reserved for an occasion where they might be more wanted.—However I quite envy you the pleasure of such a Scheme." "Oh! I am quite delighted with the thoughts of it; I can think of nothing else. I assure you I have done nothing for this last Month

---

[15] *Erased.*

but plan what Cloathes I should take with me, and I have at last determined to take very few indeed besides my travelling Dress, and so I advise you to do, when ever you go; for I intend in case we should fall in with any races, or stop at Matlock or Scarborough, to have some Things made for the occasion."

"You intend then to go into Yorkshire?"

"I beleive not—indeed I know nothing of the Route, for I never trouble myself about such things. I only know that we are to go from Derbyshire to Matlock and Scarborough, but to which of them first, I neither know nor care—I am in hopes of meeting some particular freinds of mine at Scarborough—Augusta told me in her last Letter that Sir Peter talked of going; but then you know that is so uncertain. I cannot bear Sir Peter, he is such a horrid Creature—"

"He *is,* is he?" said Kitty, not knowing what else to say. "Oh! he is quite Shocking." Here the Conversation was interrupted, and Kitty was left in a painful Uncertainty, as to the particulars of Sir Peter's Character; She knew only that he was Horrid and Shocking, but why, and in what, yet remained to be discovered. She could scarcely resolve what to think of her new Acquaintance; She appeared to be shamefully ignorant as to the Geography of England, if she had understood her right, and equally devoid of Taste and Information. Kitty was however unwilling to decide hastily; she was at once desirous of doing Miss Stanley justice, and of having her own Wishes in her answered; she determined therefore to suspend all Judgement for some time. After Supper, the Conversation turning on the state of Affairs in the political World, Mrs P, who was firmly of opinion that the whole race of Mankind were degenerating, said that for her part, Everything she beleived was going to rack and ruin, all order was destroyed over the face of the World, The house of Commons she heard did not break up sometimes till five in the Morning, and Depravity never was so general before; concluding with a wish that she might live to see the Manners of the People in Queen Elizabeth's reign, restored again. "Well Ma'am, said her Neice, [I beleive you have as good a chance of it as any one else][16] but I hope you do not mean with the times to restore Queen Elizth herself."

"Queen Elizth, said Mrs Stanley who never hazarded a remark on History that was not well founded, lived to a good old age, and was a very Clever Woman." "True Ma'am, said Kitty; but I do not consider either of those Circumstances as meritorious in herself, and they are very far from making me wish her return, for if she were to come again with the same Abilities and the same good Constitution She might do as much Mischief and last as long as she did before—then turning to Camilla who had been sitting very silent for some time, she added, What do *you* think of Elizabeth Miss Stanley? I hope you will not defend her."

"Oh! dear, said Miss Stanley, I know nothing of Politics, and cannot bear to hear them mentioned." Kitty started at this repulse, but made no answer; that Miss Stan-

---

[16] *Erased.*

ley must be ignorant of what she could not distinguish from Politics she felt perfectly convinced.—She retired to her own room, perplexed in her opinion about her new Acquaintance, and fearful of her being very unlike Cecilia and Mary. She arose the next morning to experience a fuller conviction of this, and every future day encreased it—. She found no variety in her conversation; She received no information from her but in fashions, and no Amusement but in her performance on the Harpsichord; and after repeated endeavours to find her what she wished, she was obliged to give up the attempt and to consider it as fruitless. There had occasionally appeared a something like humour in Camilla which had inspired her with hopes, that she might at least have a natural genius, tho' not an improved one, but these Sparklings of Wit happened so seldom, and were so ill-supported that she was at last convinced of their being merely accidental. All her stock of knowledge was exhausted in a very few Days, and when Kitty had learnt from her, how large their house in Town was, when the fashionable Amusements began, who were the celebrated Beauties and who the best Millener, Camilla had nothing further to teach, except the Characters of any of her Acquaintance as they occurred in Conversation, which was done with equal Ease and Brevity, by saying that the person was either the sweetest Creature in the world, and one of whom she was doatingly fond, or horrid, shocking and not fit to be seen.

As Catherine was very desirous of gaining every possible information as to the Characters of the Halifax Family, and concluded that Miss Stanley must be acquainted with them, as she seemed to be so with every one of any Consequence, she took an opportunity as Camilla was one day enumerating all the people of rank that her Mother visited, of asking her whether Lady Halifax were among the number.

"Oh! Thank you for reminding me of her, She is the sweetest Woman in the world, and one of our most intimate Acquaintances, I do not suppose there is a day passes during the six Months that we are in Town, but what we see each other in the course of it—. And I correspond with all the Girls."

"They *are* then a very pleasant Family? said Kitty. They ought to be so indeed, to allow of such frequent Meetings, or all Conversation must be at end."

"Oh! dear, not at all, said Miss Stanley, for sometimes we do not speak to each other for a month together. We meet perhaps only in Public, and then you know we are often not able to get near enough; but in that case we always nod & smile."

"Which does just as well—. But I was going to ask you whether you have ever seen a Miss Wynne with them?"

"I know who you mean perfectly—she wears a blue hat—. I have frequently seen her in Brook Street, when I have been at Lady Halifax's Balls—She gives one every Month during the Winter—. But only think how good it is in her to take care of Miss Wynne, for she is a very distant relation, and so poor that, as Miss Halifax told me, her Mother was obliged to find her in Cloathes. Is not it shameful?"

"That she should be so poor? it is indeed, with such wealthy connexions as the Family have."

"Oh! no; I mean, was not it shameful in Mr Wynne to leave his Children so distressed, when he had actually the Living of Chetwynde and two or three Curacies, and only four Children to provide for—. What would he have done if he had had ten, as many people have?"

"He would have given them all a good Education and have left them all equally poor."

"Well I do think there never was so lucky a Family. Sir George Fitzgibbon you know sent the eldest girl to India entirely at his own Expence, where they say she is most nobly married and the happiest Creature in the World—Lady Halifax you see has taken care of the youngest and treats her as if she were her Daughter; She does not go out into Public with her to be sure; but then she is always present when her Ladyship gives her Balls, and nothing can be kinder to her than Lady Halifax is; she would have taken her to Cheltenham last year, if there had been room enough at the Lodgings, and therefore I dont think that *she* can have anything to complain of. Then there are the two Sons; one of them the Bishop of M—— has got into the Army[17] as a Leiutenant I suppose; and the other is extremely well off I know, for I have a notion that somebody puts him to School somewhere in Wales. Perhaps you knew them when they lived here?"

"Very well, We met as often as your Family and the Halifaxes do in Town, but as we seldom had any difficulty in getting near enough to speak, we seldom parted with merely a Nod & a Smile. They were indeed a most charming Family, and I beleive have scarcely their Equals in the World; The Neighbours we now have at the Parsonage, appear to more disadvantage in coming after them."

"Oh! horrid Wretches! I wonder you can endure them."

"Why, what would you have one do?"

"Oh! Lord, If I were in your place, I should abuse them all day long."

"So I do, but it does no good."

"Well, I declare it is quite a pity that they should be suffered to live. I wish my Father would propose knocking all their Brains out, some day or other when he is in the House. So abominably proud of their Family! And I dare say after all, that there is nothing particular in it."

"Why Yes, I beleive thay *have* reason to value themselves on it, if any body has; for you know he is Lord Amyatt's Brother."

"Oh! I know all that very well, but it is no reason for their being so horrid. I remember I met Miss Dudley last Spring with Lady Amyatt at Ranelagh, and she had such a frightful Cap on, that I have never been able to bear any of them since.—And so you used to think the Wynnes very pleasant?" "You speak as if their being so were doubtful! Pleasant! Oh! they were every thing that could interest and attach. It is not in my power to do Justice to their Merits, tho' not to feel them, I think must be impossible.

---

[17] sent to Sea *erased.*

They have unfitted me for any Society but their own!"

"Well, That is just what I think of the Miss Halifaxes; by the bye, I must write to Caroline tomorrow, and I do not know what to say to her. The Barlows too are just such other sweet Girls; but I wish Augusta's hair was not so dark. I cannot bear Sir Peter—Horrid Wretch! He is *always* laid up with the Gout, which is exceedingly disagreeable to the Family."

"And perhaps not very pleasant to *himself*—. But as to the Wynnes; do you really think them very fortunate?"

"Do I? Why, does not every body? Miss Halifax & Caroline & Maria all say that they are the luckiest Creatures in the World. So does Sir George Fitzgibbon and so do Every body."

"That is, Every body who have themselves conferred an obligation on them. But do you call it lucky, for a Girl of Genius & Feeling to be sent in quest of a Husband to Bengal, to be married there to a Man of whose Disposition she has no opportunity of judging till her Judgement is of no use to her, who may be a Tyrant, or a Fool or both for what she knows to the Contrary. Do you call *that* fortunate?"

"I know nothing of all that; I only know that it was extremely good in Sir George to fit her out and pay her Passage, and that she would not have found Many who would have done the same."

"I wish she had not found *one,* said Kitty with great Eagerness, she might then have remained in England and been happy."

"Well, I cannot conceive the hardship of going out in a very agreeable Manner with two or three sweet Girls for Companions, having a delightful voyage to Bengal or Barbadoes or wherever it is, and being married soon after one's arrival to a very charming Man immensely rich—. I see no hardship in all that."

"Your representation of the Affair, said Kitty laughing, certainly gives a very different idea of it from Mine. But supposing all this to be true, still, as it was by no means certain that she would be so fortunate either in her voyage, her Companions, or her husband; in being obliged to run the risk of their proving very different, she undoubtedly experienced a great hardship—. Besides, to a Girl of any Delicacy, the voyage in itself, since the object of it is so universally known, is a punishment that needs no other to make it very severe.'

"I do not see that at all. She is not the first Girl who has gone to the East Indies for a Husband, and I declare I should think it very good fun if I were as poor."

"I beleive you would think very differently *then.* But at least you will not defend her Sister's situation? Dependant even for her Cloathes on the bounty of others, who of course do not pity her, as by your own account, they consider her as very fortunate."

"You are extremely nice upon my word; Lady Halifax is a delightful Woman, and one of the sweetest tempered Creatures in the World; I am sure I have every reason to speak well of her, for we are under most amazing Obligations to her. She has frequently chaperoned me when my Mother has been indisposed, and last Spring she lent me her own horse three times, which was a prodigious favour, for it is the most beautiful Creature that ever was seen, and I am the only person she ever lent it to.

["If so, *Mary Wynne* can receive very little advantage from her having it."][18]

And then, continued she, the Miss Halifaxes are quite delightful. Maria is one of the cleverest Girls that ever were known—Draws in Oils, and plays anything by sight. She promised me one of her Drawings before I left Town, but I entirely forgot to ask her for it. I would give anything to have one." [Why indeed, if Maria will give my Freind a drawing, she can have nothing to complain of, but as she does not write in Spirits, I suppose she has not yet been fortunate enough to be so distinguished.][19] "But was not it very odd, said Kitty, that the Bishop should send Charles Wynne to sea, when he must have had a much better chance of providing for him in the Church, which was the profession that Charles liked best, and the one for which his Father had intended him? The Bishop I know had often promised Mr Wynne a living, and as he never gave him one, I think it was incumbant on him to transfer the promise to his Son."

"I beleive you think he ought to have resigned his Bishopric to him; you seem determined to be dissatisfied with every thing that has been done for them."

"Well, said Kitty, this is a subject on which we shall never agree, and therefore it will be useless to continue it farther, or to mention it again—" She then left the room, and running out of the House was soon in her dear Bower where she could indulge in peace all her affectionate Anger against the relations of the Wynnes, which was greatly heightened by finding from Camilla that they were in general considered as having acted particularly well by them—. She amused herself for some time in Abusing, and Hating them all, with great spirit, and when this tribute to her regard for the Wynnes, was paid, and the Bower began to have its usual influence over her Spirits, she contributed towards settling them, by taking out a book, for she had always one about her, and reading—. She had been so employed for nearly an hour, when Camilla came running towards her with great Eagerness, and apparently great Pleasure—. "Oh! my Dear Catherine, said she, half out of Breath—I have such delightful News for You—But you shall guess what it is—We are all the happiest Creatures in the World; would you beleive it, the Dudleys have sent us an invitation to a Ball at their own House—. What Charming People they are! I had no idea of there being so much sense in the whole Family—I declare I quite doat upon them—. And it happens so fortunately too, for I expect a new Cap from Town tomorrow which will just do for a Ball—Gold Net—It will be a most angelic thing—Every Body will be longing for the pattern—" The expectation of a Ball was indeed very agreable intelligence to Kitty, who fond of Dancing and seldom able to enjoy it, had reason to feel even greater pleasure in it than her Freind; for to *her*, it was now no novelty—. Camilla's delight how-

---

18 *Erased.*

19 *Erased.*

ever was by no means inferior to Kitty's, and she rather expressed the most of the two. The Cap came and every other preparation was soon completed; while these were in agitation the Days passed gaily away, but when Directions were no longer necessary, Taste could no longer be displayed, and Difficulties no longer overcome, the short period that intervened before the day of the Ball hung heavily on their hands, and every hour was too long. The very few Times that Kitty had ever enjoyed the Amusement of Dancing was an excuse for *her* impatience, and an apology for the Idleness it occasioned to a Mind naturally very Active; but her Freind without such a plea was infinitely worse than herself. She could do nothing but wander from the house to the Garden, and from the Garden to the avenue, wondering when Thursday would come, which she might easily have ascertained, and counting the hours as they passed which served only to lengthen them.—. They retired to their rooms in high Spirits on Wednesday night, but Kitty awoke the next Morning with a violent Toothake. It was in vain that she endeavoured at first to deceive herself; her feelings were witnesses too acute of it's reality; with as little success did she try to sleep it off, for the pain she suffered prevented her closing her Eyes—. She then summoned her Maid and with the Assistance of the Housekeeper, every remedy that the receipt book or the head of the latter contained, was tried, but ineffectually; for though for a short time releived by them, the pain still returned. She was now obliged to give up the endeavour, and to reconcile herself not only to the pain of a Toothake, but to the loss of a Ball; and though she had with so much eagerness looked forward to the day of its arrival, had received such pleasure in the necessary preparations, and promised herself so much delight in it, Yet she was not so totally void of philosophy as many Girls of her age, might have been in her situation. She considered that there were Misfortunes of a much greater magnitude than the loss of a Ball, experienced every day by some part of Mortality, and that the time might come when She would herself look back with Wonder and perhaps with Envy on her having known no greater vexation. By such reflections as these, she soon reasoned herself into as much Resignation & Patience as the pain she suffered, would allow of, which after all was the greatest Misfortune of the two, and told the sad story when she entered the Breakfast room, with tolerable Composure. Mrs Percival more grieved for her toothake than her Disappointment, as she feared that it would not be possible to prevent her Dancing with a *Man* if she went, was eager to try everything that had already been applied to alleviate the pain, while at the same time She declared it was impossible for her to leave the House. Miss Stanley who joined to her concern for her Freind, felt a mixture of Dread lest her Mother's proposal that they should all remain at home, might be accepted, was very violent in her sorrow on the occasion, and though her apprehensions on the subject were soon quieted by Kitty's protesting that sooner than allow any one to stay with her, she would herself go, she continued to lament it with such unceasing vehemence as at last drove Kitty to her own room. Her Fears for herself being now entirely dissipated left her more than ever at leisure to pity and persecute her Freind who tho' safe when in her own room, was frequently removing from it to some other in hopes of being more free from pain, and then had no opportunity of escaping her—.

"To be sure, there never was anything so shocking, said Camilla; To come on such a day too! For one would not have minded it you know had it been at *any other* time. But it always is so. I never was at a Ball in my Life, but what something happened to prevent somebody from going! I wish there were no such things as Teeth in the World; they are nothing but plagues to one, and I dare say that People might easily invent something to eat with instead of them; Poor Thing! what pain you are in! I declare it is quite Shocking to look at you. But you wo'nt have it out, will you? For Heaven's sake do'nt; for there is nothing I dread so much. I declare I had rather undergo the greatest Tortures in the World than have a tooth drawn. Well! how patiently you do bear it! how can you be so quiet? Lord, if I were in your place I should make such a fuss, there would be no bearing me. I should torment you to Death."

"So you do, as it is," thought Kitty.

"For my own part, Catherine said Mrs Percival I have not a doubt but that you caught this toothake by sitting so much in that Arbour, for it is always damp. I know it has ruined your Constitution entirely; and indeed I do not beleive it has been of much service to mine; I sate down in it last May to rest myself, and I have never been quite well since—. I shall order John to pull it all down I assure you."

"I know you will not do that Ma'am, said Kitty, as you must be convinced how unhappy it would make me."

"You talk very ridiculously Child; it is all whim & Nonsense. Why cannot you fancy this room an Arbour?

"Had this room been built by Cecilia & Mary, I should have valued it equally Ma'am, for it is not merely the name of an Arbour, which charms me."

"Why indeed Mrs Percival, said Mrs Stanley, I must think that Catherine's affection for her Bower is the effect of a Sensibility that does her Credit. I love to see a Freindship between young Persons and always consider it as a sure mark of an aimiable affectionate disposition. I have from Camilla's infancy taught her to think the same, and have taken great pains to introduce her to young people of her own age who were likely to be worthy of her regard. [There is something mighty pretty I think in young Ladies corresponding with each other, and][20] nothing forms the taste more than sensible & Elegant Letters—. Lady Halifax thinks just like me—. Camilla corresponds with her Daughters, and I beleive I may venture to say that they are none of them *the worse* for it." These ideas were too modern to suit Mrs Percival who considered a correspondence between Girls as productive of no good, and as the frequent origin of imprudence & Error by the effect of pernicious advice and bad Example. She could not therefore refrain from saying that for her part, she had lived fifty Years in the world without having ever had a correspondent, and did not find herself at all

[20] *Erased.*

the less respectable for it—. Mrs Stanley could say nothing in answer to this, but her Daughter who was less governed by Propriety, said in her thoughtless way, "But who knows what you might have been Ma'am, if you *had* had a Correspondent; perhaps it would have made you quite a different Creature. I declare I would not be without those I have for all the World. It is the greatest delight of my Life, and you cannot think how much their Letters have formed my taste as Mama says, for I hear from them generally every week."

"You received a Letter from Augusta Barlow to day, did not you my Love? said her Mother—. She writes remarkably well I know."

"Oh! Yes Ma'am, the most delightful Letter you ever heard of. She sends me a long account of the new Regency walking dress Lady Susan has given her, and it is so beautiful that I am quite dieing with envy for it."

"Well, I am prodigiously happy to hear such pleasing news of my young freind; I have a high regard for Augusta, and most sincerely partake in the general Joy on the occasion. But does she say nothing else? it seemed to be a long Letter—Are they to be at Scarborough?"

"Oh! Lord, she never once mentions it, now I recollect it; and I entirely forgot to ask her when I wrote last. She says nothing indeed except about the Regency." "She *must* write well thought Kitty, to make a long Letter upon a Bonnet & Pelisse." She then left the room tired of listening to a conversation which tho' it might have diverted her had she been well, served only to fatigue and depress her, while in pain. Happy was it for *her*, when the hour of dressing came, for Camilla satisfied with being surrounded by her Mother and half the Maids in the House did not want her assistance, and was too agreably employed to want her Society. She remained therefore alone in the parlour, till joined by Mr Stanley & her Aunt, who however after a few enquiries, allowed her to continue undisturbed and began their usual conversation on Politics. This was a subject on which they could never agree, for Mr Stanley who considered himself as perfectly qualified by his Seat in the House, to decide on it without hesitation, resolutely maintained that the Kingdom had not for ages been in so flourishing & prosperous a state, and Mrs Percival with equal warmth, tho' perhaps less argument, as vehemently asserted that the whole Nation would speedily be ruined, and everything as she expressed herself be at sixes & sevens. It was not however unamusing to Kitty to listen to the Dispute, especially as she began then to be more free from pain, and without taking any share in it herself, she found it very entertaining to observe the eagerness with which they both defended their opinions, and could not help thinking that Mr Stanley would not feel more disappointed if her Aunt's expectations were fulfilled, than her Aunt would be mortified by their failure. After waiting a considerable time Mrs Stanley & her daughter appeared, and Camilla in high Spirits, & perfect good humour with her own looks, was more violent than ever in her lamentations over her Freind as she practised her scotch Steps about the room—. At length they departed, & Kitty better able to amuse herself than she had been the whole Day before, wrote a long account of her Misfortunes to Mary Wynne. When her Letter was concluded she had an opportunity of witnessing the truth of that assertion which says that Sorrows are lightened by Communication, for her toothake was then so much releived that she began to entertain an idea of following her Freinds to Mr Dudley's. They had been gone an hour, and as every thing relative to her Dress was in complete readiness, She considered that in another hour since there was so little a way to go, She might be there—. They were gone in Mr Stanley's Carriage and therefore She might follow in her Aunt's. As the plan seemed so very easy to be executed, and promising so much pleasure, it was after a few Minutes deliberation finally adopted, and running up stairs, She rang in great haste for her Maid. The Bustle & Hurry which then ensued for nearly an hour was at last happily concluded by her finding herself very well-dressed and in high Beauty. Anne was then dispatched in the same haste to order the Carriage, while her Mistress was putting on her gloves, & arranging the folds of her dress, [and providing herself with Lavender water].[21] In a few Minutes she heard the Carriage drive up to the Door, and tho' at first surprised at the expedition with which it had been got ready, she concluded after a little reflection that the Men had received some hint of her intentions beforehand, and was hastening out of the room, when Anne came running into it in the greatest hurry and agitation, exclaiming "Lord Ma'am! Here's a Gentleman in a Chaise and four come, and I cannot for my Life conceive who it is! I happened to be crossing the hall when the Carriage drove up, and as I knew nobody would be in the way to let him in but Tom, and he looks so awkward you know Ma'am, now his hair is just done up, that I was not willing the gentleman should see him, and so I went to the door myself. And he is one of the handsomest young Men you would wish to see; I was almost ashamed of being seen in my Apron Ma'am, but however he is vastly handsome and did not seem to mind it at all.—And he asked me whether the Family were at home; and so I said everybody was gone out but you Ma'am, for I would not deny you because I was sure you would like to see him. And then he asked me whether Mr and Mrs Stanley were not here, and so I said Yes, and then——

"Good Heavens! said Kitty, what can all this mean! And who can it possibly be! Did you never see him before? And Did not he tell you his Name?"

"No Ma'am, he never said anything about it—So then I asked him to walk into the parlour, and he was prodigious agreable, and——

"Whoever he is, said her Mistress, he has made a great impression upon you Nanny—But where did he come from? and what does he want here?

"Oh! Ma'am, I was going to tell you, that I fancy his business is with you; for he asked me whether you were at leisure to see anybody, and desired I would give his Compliments to you, & say he should be very happy to wait on you—However I thought he had better not come up into your Dressing room, especially as everything

[21] *Erased.*

is in such a litter, so I told him if he would be so obliging as to stay in the parlour, I would run up stairs and tell you he was come, and I dared to say that you would wait upon *him*. Lord Ma'am, I'd lay anything that he is come to ask you to dance with him tonight, & has got his Chaise ready to take you to Mr Dudley's."

Kitty could not help laughing at this idea, & only wished it might be true, as it was very likely that she would be too late for any other partner—"But what, in the name of wonder, can he have to say to me? Perhaps he is come to rob the house—he comes in stile at least; and it will be some consolation for our losses to be robbed by a Gentleman in a Chaise & 4—. What Livery has his Servants?"

"Why that is the most wonderful thing about him Ma'am, for he has not a single servant with him, and came with hack horses; But he is as handsome as a Prince for all that, and has quite the look of one. Do dear Ma'am, go down, for I am sure you will be delighted with him—"

"Well, I beleive I must go; but it is very odd! What can he have to say to me." Then giving one look at herself in the Glass, she walked with great impatience, tho' trembling all the while from not knowing what to expect, down Stairs, and after pausing a moment at the door to gather Courage for opening it, she resolutely entered the room. The Stranger, whose appearance did not disgrace the account she had received of it from her Maid, rose up on her entrance, and laying aside the Newspaper he had been reading, advanced towards her with an air of the most perfect Ease & Vivacity, and said to her, "It is certainly a very awkward circumstance to be thus obliged to introduce myself, but I trust that the necessity of the case will plead my Excuse, and prevent your being prejudiced by it against me—. *Your* name, I need not ask Ma'am—. Miss Percival is too well known to me by description to need any information of that." Kitty, who had been expecting him to tell his own name, instead of hers, and who from having been little in company, and never before in such a situation, felt herself unable to ask it, tho' she had been planning her speech all the way down stairs, was so confused & distressed by this unexpected address that she could only return a slight curtesy to it, and accepted the chair he reached her, without knowing what she did. The gentleman then continued. "You are, I dare say, surprised to see me returned from France so soon, and nothing indeed but business could have brought me to England; a very Melancholy affair has now occasioned it, and I was unwilling to leave it without paying my respects to the Family in Devonshire whom I have so long wished to be acquainted with—." Kitty, who felt much more surprised at his supposing her *to be so,* than at seeing a person in England, whose having ever left it was perfectly unknown to her, still continued silent from Wonder & Perplexity, and her visitor still continued to talk. "You will suppose Madam that I was not the *less* desirous of waiting on you, from your having Mr & Mrs Stanley with you—. I hope they are well? And Mrs Percival how does *she* do?" Then without waiting for an answer he gaily added, "But my dear Miss Percival you are going out I am sure; and I am detaining you from your appointment. How can I ever expect to be forgiven for such injustice! Yet how can I, so circumstanced, forbear to offend! You seem dressed for a Ball? But this is the Land of gaiety I know; I have for many years been desirous of visiting it. You have Dances I suppose at least every week—But where are the rest of your party gone, and what kind Angel in compassion to me, has excluded *you* from it?"

"Perhaps Sir, said Kitty extremely confused by his manner of speaking to her, and highly displeased with the freedom of his Conversation towards one who had never seen him before and did not *now* know his name, "perhaps Sir, you are acquainted with Mr & Mrs Stanley; and your business may be with *them*?"

"You do me too much honour Ma'am, replied he laughing, in supposing me to be acquainted with Mr & Mrs Stanley; I merely know them by sight; very distant relations; only my Father & Mother. Nothing more I assure you."

"Gracious Heaven! said Kitty, are *you* Mr Stanley then?—I beg a thousand pardons—Though really upon recollection I do not know for what—for you never told me your name——"

"I beg your pardon—I made a very fine speech when you entered the room, all about introducing myself; I assure you it was very great for *me*."

"The speech had certainly great Merit, said Kitty smiling; I thought so at the time; but since you never mentioned your name in it, as an *introductory one* it might have been better."

There was such an air of good humour and Gaiety in Stanley, that Kitty, tho' perhaps not authorized to address him with so much familiarity on so short an acquaintance, could not forbear indulging the natural Unreserve & Vivacity of her own Disposition, in speaking to him, as he spoke to her. She was intimately acquainted too with his Family who were her relations, and she chose to consider herself entitled by the connexion to forget how little a while they had known each other. "Mr & Mrs Stanley and your Sister are extremely well, said she, and will I dare say be very much surprised to see you—But I am sorry to hear that your return to England has been occasioned by an unpleasant circumstance."

"Oh, Do'nt talk of it, said he, it is a most confounded shocking affair, & makes me miserable to think of it; But where are my Father & Mother, & your Aunt gone? Oh! Do you know that I met the prettiest little waiting maid in the world, when I came here; she let me into the house; I took her for you at first."

"You did me a great deal of honour, and give me more credit for good nature than I deserve, for I *never* go to the door when any one comes."

"Nay do not be angry; I mean no offence. But tell me, where are you going to so smart? Your carriage is just coming round."

"I am going to a Dance at a Neighbour's, where your Family and my Aunt are already gone."

"Gone, without you! what's the meaning of *that*? But I suppose you are like myself, rather long in dressing."

"I must have been so indeed, if that were the case for they have been gone nearly these two hours; The reason however was not what you suppose—I was prevented going by a pain——

"By a pain! interrupted Stanley, Oh! heavens, that is dreadful indeed! No Matter where the pain was. But my dear Miss Percival, what do you say to my accompanying you? And suppose you were to dance with me too? *I* think it would be very pleasant."

"I can have no objection to either I am sure, said Kitty laughing to find how near the truth her Maid's conjecture had been; on the contrary I shall be highly honoured by both, and I can answer for Your being extremely welcome to the Family who give the Ball."

"Oh! hang them; who cares for that; they cannot turn me out of the house. But I am afraid I shall cut a sad figure among all your Devonshire Beaux in this dusty, travelling apparel, and I have not wherewithal to change it. You can procure me some powder perhaps, and I must get a pair of Shoes from one of the Men, for I was in such a devil of a hurry to leave Lyons that I had not time to have anything pack'd up but some linen." Kitty very readily undertook to procure for him everything he wanted, & telling the footman to shew him into Mr Stanley's dressing room, gave Nanny orders to send in some powder & pomatum, which orders Nanny chose to execute in person. As Stanley's preparations in dressing were confined to such very trifling articles, Kitty of course expected him in about ten minutes; but she found that it had not been merely a boast of vanity in saying that he was dilatory in that respect, as he kept her waiting for him above half an hour, so that the Clock had struck ten before he entered the room and the rest of the party had gone by eight.

"Well, said he as he came in, have not I been very quick? I never hurried so much in my Life before."

"In that case you certainly have, replied Kitty, for all Merit you know is comparative."

"Oh! I knew you would be delighted with me for making so must[22] haste—. But come, the Carriage is ready; so, do not keep me waiting." And so saying he took her by the hand, & led her out of the room. "Why, my dear Cousin, said he when they were seated, this will be a most agreable surprize to everybody to see you enter the room with such a smart Young Fellow as I am—I hope your Aunt won't be alarmed."

"To tell you the truth, replied Kitty, I think the best way to prevent it, will be to send for her, or your Mother before we go into the room, especially as you are a perfect stranger, & must of course be introduced to Mr & Mrs Dudley—"

"Oh! Nonsense, said he; I did not expect *you* to stand upon such Ceremony; Our acquaintance with each other renders all such Prudery, ridiculous; Besides, if we go in together, we shall be the whole talk of the Country—"

"To *me* replied Kitty, that would certainly be a most powerful inducement; but I scarcely know whether my Aunt would consider it as such—. Women at her time of life, have odd ideas of propriety you know."

---

22 *sic.*

"Which is the very thing that you ought to break them of; and why should you object to entering a room with me where all our relations are, when you have done me the honour to admit me without any chaprone into your Carriage? Do not you think your Aunt will be as much offended with you for one, as for the other of these mighty crimes."

"Why really said Catherine, I do not know but that she may; however, it is no reason that I should offend against Decorum a second time, because I have already done it once."

"On the contrary, that is the very reason which makes it impossible for you to prevent it, since you cannot offend for the *first time* again."

"You are very ridiculous, said she laughing, but I am afraid your arguments divert me too much to convince me."

"At least they will convince you that I am very agreable, which after all, is the happiest conviction for me, and as to the affair of Propriety we will let that rest till we arrive at our Journey's end—. This is a monthly Ball I suppose. Nothing but Dancing here—."

"I thought I had told you that it was given by a Mr Dudley—"

"Oh! aye so you did; but why should not Mr Dudley give one every month? By the bye who *is that* Man? Everybody gives Balls now I think; I beleive I must give one myself soon—. Well, but how do you like my Father & Mother? And poor little Camilla too, has not she plagued you to death with the Halifaxes?" Here the Carriage fortunately stopped at Mr Dudley's, and Stanley was too much engaged in handing her out of it, to wait for an answer, or to remember that what he had said required one. They entered the small vestibule which Mr Dudley had raised to the Dignity of a Hall, & Kitty immediately desired the footman who was leading the way upstairs, to inform either Mrs Peterson, or Mrs Stanley of her arrival, & beg them to come to her, but Stanley unused to any contradiction & impatient to be amongst them, would neither allow her to wait, or listen to what she said, & forcibly seizing her arm within his, overpowered her voice with the rapidity of his own, & Kitty half angry & half laughing was obliged to go with him up stairs, and could even with difficulty prevail on him to relinquish her hand before they entered the room. Mrs Percival was at that very moment engaged in conversation with a Lady at the upper end of the room, to whom she had been giving a long account of her Neice's unlucky disappointment, & the dreadful pain that she had with so much fortitude, endured the whole Day—"I left her however, said she, thank heaven!, a little better, and I hope she has been able to amuse herself with a book, poor thing! for she must otherwise be very dull. She is probably in bed by this time, which while she is so poorly, is the best place for her you know Ma'am." The Lady was going to give her assent to this opinion, when the Noise of voices on the stairs, and the footman's opening the door as if for the entrance of Company, attracted the attention of every body in the room; and as it was in one of those Intervals between the Dances when every one seemed glad to sit down, Mrs Peterson had a most unfortunate opportunity of seeing her Neice whom she had supposed in bed, or amusing herself as the height of gaity with a book, enter the room most elegantly dressed, with a smile on her Countenance, and a glow of mingled Chearfulness & Confusion on her Cheeks, attended by a young Man uncommonly handsome, and who without any of her Confusion, appeared to have all her vivacity. Mrs Percival colouring with anger & astonishment, rose from her Seat, & Kitty walked eagerly towards her, impatient to account for what she saw appeared wonderful to every body, and extremely offensive to *her*, while Camilla on seeing her Brother ran instantly towards him, and very soon explained who he was by her words & her actions. Mr Stanley, who so fondly doated on his Son, that the pleasure of seeing him again after an absence of three Months prevented his feeling for the time any anger against him for returning to England without his knowledge, received him with equal surprise & delight; and soon comprehending the cause of his Journey, forbore any further conversation with him, as he was eager to see his Mother, & it was necessary that he should be introduced to Mr Dudley's family. This introduction to any one but Stanley would have been highly unpleasant, for they considered their dignity injured by his coming uninvited to their house, & received him with more than their usual haughtiness: But Stanley who with a vivacity of temper seldom subdued, & a contempt of censure not to be overcome, possessed an opinion of his own Consequence, & a perseverance in his own schemes which were not to be damped by the conduct of others, appeared not to perceive it. The Civilities therefore which they coldly offered, he received with a gaiety & ease peculiar to himself, and then attended by his Father & Sister walked into another room where his Mother was playing at Cards, to experience another Meeting, and undergo a repetition of pleasure, surprise, & Explanations. While these were passing, Camilla eager to communicate all she felt to some one who would attend to her, returned to Catherine, & seating herself by her, immediately began—"Well, did you ever know anything so delightful as this? But it always is so; I never go to a Ball in my Life but what something or other happens unexpectedly that is quite charming!"

"A Ball replied Kitty, seems to be a most eventful thing to you—"

"Oh! Lord, it is indeed—But only think of my brother's returning so suddenly—And how shocking a thing it is that has brought him over! I never heard anything so dreadful—!"

"What is it pray that has occasioned his leaving France? I am sorry to find that it is a melancholy event."

"Oh! it is beyond anything you can conceive! His favourite Hunter who was turned out in the park on his going abroad, somehow or other fell ill—No, I beleive it was an accident, but however it was something or other, or else it was something else, and so they sent an Express immediately to Lyons where my Brother was, for they knew that he valued this Mare more than anything else in the World besides; and so my Brother set off directly for England, and without packing up another Coat; I am quite angry with him about it; it was so shocking you know to come away without a change of Cloathes—"

"Why indeed said Kitty, it seems to have been a very shocking affair from beginning to end."

"Oh! it is beyond anything You can conceive! I would rather have had *anything* happen than that he should have lossed that mare."

"Except his coming away without another coat."

"Oh! yes, that has vexed me more than you can imagine.— Well, & so Edward got to Brampton just as the poor Thing was dead; but as he could not bear to remain there *then,* he came off directly to Chetwynde on purpose to see us—. I hope he may not go abroad again."

"Do you think he will not?"

"Oh! dear, to be sure he must, but I wish he may not with all my heart—. You cannot think how fond I am of him! By the bye are not you in love with him yourself?"

"To be sure I am replied Kitty laughing, I am in love with every handsome Man I see."

"That is just like me—*I* am always in love with every handsome Man in the World."

"There you outdo me replied Catherine for I am only in love with those I *do* see." Mrs Percival who was sitting on the other side of her, & who began now to distinguish the words, *Love* & *handsome Man,* turned hastily towards them, & said "What are you talking of Catherine?" To which Catherine immediately answered with the simple artifice of a Child, "Nothing Ma'am." She had already received a very severe lecture from her Aunt on the imprudence of her behaviour during the whole evening; She blamed her for coming to the Ball, for coming in the same Carriage with Edward Stanley, and still more for entering the room with him. For the last-mentioned offence Catherine knew not what apology to give, and tho' she longed in answer to the second to say that she had not thought it would be civil to make Mr Stanley *walk,* she dared not so to trifle with her aunt, who would have been but the more offended by it. The first accusation however she considered as very unreasonable, as she thought herself perfectly justified in coming. This conversation continued till Edward Stanley entering the room came instantly towards her, and telling her that every one waited for *her* to begin the next Dance led her to the top of the room, for Kitty impatient to escape from so unpleasant a Companion, without the least hesitation, or one civil scruple at being so distinguished, immediately gave him her hand, & joyfully left her seat. This Conduct however was highly resented by several young Ladies present, and among the rest by Miss Stanley whose regard for her brother tho' *excessive,* & whose affection for Kitty tho' *prodigious,* were not proof against such an injury to her importance and her peace. Edward had however only consulted his own inclinations in desiring Miss Peterson to begin the Dance, nor had he any reason to know that it was either wished or expected by anyone else in the Party. As an heiress she was certainly of consequence, but her Birth gave her no other claim to it, for her Father had been a Merchant. It was this very circumstance which rendered this unfortunate affair so offensive to Camilla, for tho' she would sometimes boast in the pride of her heart, & her eagerness to be admired that she did not know who her grandfather had been, and was as ignorant of everything relative to Genealogy as to Astronomy, (and she might have added, Geography) yet she was really proud of her family & Connexions, and easily offended if they were treated with Neglect. "I should not have minded it, said she to her Mother, if she had been *anybody* else's daughter; but to see her pretend to be above *me,* when her Father was only a tradesman, is too bad! It is such an affront to our whole Family! I declare I think Papa ought to interfere in it, but he never cares about anything but Politics. If I were Mr Pitt or the Lord Chancellor, he would take care I should not be insulted, but he never thinks about *me;* And it is so provoking that *Edward* should let her stand there. I wish with all my heart that he had never come to England! I hope she may fall down & break her neck, or sprain her Ancle." Mrs Stanley perfectly agreed with her daughter concerning the affair, & tho' with less violence, expressed almost equal resentment at the indignity. Kitty in the meantime remained insensible of having given any one Offence, and therefore unable either to offer an apology, or make a reparation; her whole attention was occupied by the happiness she enjoyed in dancing with the most elegant young Man in the room, and every one else was equally unregarded. The Evening indeed to *her,* passed off delightfully; he was her partner during the greatest part of it, and the united attractions that he possessed of Person, Address & vivacity, had easily gained that preference from Kitty which they seldom fail of obtaining from every one. She was too happy to care either for her Aunt's illhumour which she could not help remarking, or for the Alteration in Camilla's behaviour which forced itself at last on her observation. Her Spirits were elevated above the influence of Displeasure in any one, and she was equally indifferent as to the cause of Camilla's, or the continuance of her Aunt's. Though Mr Stanley could never be really offended by any imprudence or folly in his Son that had given him the pleasure of seeing him, he was yet perfectly convinced that Edward ought not to remain in England, and was resolved to hasten his leaving it as soon as possible; but when he talked to Edward about it, he found him much less disposed towards returning to France, than to accompany them in their projected tour, which he assured his Father would be infinitely more pleasant to him, and that as to the affair of travelling he considered it of no importance, and what might be pursued at any little odd time, when he had nothing better to do. He advanced these objections in a manner which plainly shewed that he had scarcely a doubt of their being complied with, and appeared to consider his father's arguments in opposition to them, as merely given with a veiw to keep up his authority, & such as he should find little difficulty in combating. He concluded at last by saying, as the chaise in which they returned together from Mr Dudley's reached Mrs Percivals, "Well Sir, we will settle this point some other time, and fortunately it is of so little consequence, that an immediate discussion of it is unnecessary." He then got out of the chaise & entered the house without waiting for his Father's reply. It was not till their return that Kitty could account for that coldness in Camilla's behaviour to her, which had been so pointed as to render it impossible to be entirely unnoticed. When however they were seated in the Coach with the two other Ladies, Miss Stanley's indignation was no longer to be suppressed from breaking out into words, & found the following vent.

"Well, I must say *this*, that I never was at a stupider Ball in my Life! But it always is so; I am always disappointed in them for some reason or other. I wish there were no such things."

"I am sorry Miss Stanley, said Mrs Percival drawing herself up, that you have not been amused; every thing was meant for the best I am sure, and it is a poor encouragement for your Mama to take you to another if you are so hard to be satisfied."

"I do not know what you mean Ma'am about Mama's *taking* me to another. You know I am come out."

"Oh! dear Mrs Percival, said Mrs Stanley, you must not beleive everything that my lively Camilla says, for her spirits are prodigiously high sometimes, and she frequently speaks without thinking. I am sure it is impossible for *any one* to have been at a more elegant or agreable dance, and so she wishes to express herself I am certain."

"To be sure I do, said Camilla very sulkily, only I must say that it is not very pleasant to have any body behave so rude to me as to be quite shocking! I am sure I am not at all offended, and should not care if all the World were to stand above me, but still it is extremely abominable, & what I cannot put up with. It is not that I mind it in the least, for I had just as soon stand at the bottom as at the top all night long, if it was not so very disagreable—. But to have a person come in the middle of the Evening & take everybody's place is what I am not used to, and tho' I do not care a pin about it myself, I assure you I shall not easily forgive or forget it."

This speech which perfectly explained the whole affair to Kitty, was shortly followed on her side by a very submissive apology, for she had too much good Sense to be proud of her family, and too much good Nature to live at variance with any one. The Excuses she made, were delivered with so much real concern for the Offence, and such unaffected Sweetness, that it was almost impossible for Camilla to retain that anger which had occasioned them; She felt indeed most highly gratified to find that no insult had been intended and that Catherine was very far from forgetting the difference in their birth for which she could *now* only pity her, and her good humour being restored with the same Ease in which it had been affected, she spoke with the highest delight of the Evening, & declared that she had never before been at so pleasant a Ball. The same endeavours that had procured the forgiveness of Miss Stanly ensured to her the cordiality of her Mother, and nothing was wanting but Mrs P's good humour to render the happiness of the others complete; but She, offended with Camilla for her affected Superiority, Still more so with her brother for coming to Chetwynde, & dissatisfied with the whole Evening, continued silent & Gloomy and was a restraint on the vivacity of her Companions. She eagerly seized the very first opportunity which the next Morning offered to her of speaking to Mr Stanley on the subject of his son's return, and after having expressed her opinion of its being a very silly affair that he came at all, concluded with desiring him to inform Mr Edward

Stanley that it was a rule with her never to admit a young Man into her house as a visitor for any length of time.

"I do not speak Sir, she continued, out of any disrespect to You, but I could not answer it to myself to allow of his stay; there is no knowing what might be the consequence of it, if he were to continue here, for girls nowadays will always give a handsome young Man the preference before any other, tho' for why, I never could discover, for what after all is Youth and Beauty? [Why in fact, it is nothing more than being Young and Handsome—and that][23] It is but a poor substitute for real worth & Merit; Beleive me Cousin that, what ever people may say to the contrary, there is certainly nothing like Virtue for making us what we ought to be, and as to a young Man's, being young & handsome & having an agreable person, it is nothing at all to the purpose for he had much better be respectable. I always *did* think so, and I always *shall*, and therefore you will oblige me very much by desiring your son to leave Chetwynde, or I cannot be answerable for what may happen between him and my Neice. You will be surprised to hear *me* say it, she continued, lowering her voice, but truth will out, and I must own that Kitty is one of the most impudent Girls that ever existed. [Her intimacies with Young Men are abominable, and it is all the same to her, who it is, no one comes amiss to her][24] I assure you Sir, that I have seen her sit and laugh and whisper with a young Man whom she has not seen above half a dozen times. Her behaviour indeed is scandalous, and therefore I beg you will send your Son away immediately, or everything will be at sixes & sevens." Mr Stanley who from one part of her Speech had scarcely known to what length her insinuations of Kitty's impudence were meant to extend, now endeavoured to quiet her fears on the occasion, by assuring her, that on every account he meant to allow only of his son's continuing that day with them, and that she might depend on his being more earnest in the affair from a wish of obliging her. He added also that he knew Edward to be very desirous himself of returning to France, as he wisely considered all time lost that did not forward the plans in which he was at present engaged, tho' he was but too well convinced of the contrary himself. His assurance in some degree quieted Mrs P, & left her tolerably releived of her Cares & Alarms, & better disposed to behave with civility towards his Son during the short remainder of his stay at Chetwynde. Mr Stanley went immediately to Edward, to whom he repeated the Conversation that had passed between Mrs P & himself, & strongly pointed out the necessity of his leaving Chetwynde the next day, since his word was already engaged for it. His son however appeared struck only by the ridiculous apprehensions of Mrs Peterson; and highly delighted at having occasioned them himself, seemed engrossed alone in thinking how he might encrease them, without attending to any other part of his Father's Conversation. Mr Stanley could get no determinate Answer from him, and tho' he still hoped for the best, they

---

23 *erased, and* It *substituted.*

24 *Erased.*

parted almost in anger on his side. His Son though by no means disposed to marry, or any otherwise attached to Miss Percival than as a good natured lively Girl who seemed pleased with him, took infinite pleasure in alarming the jealous fears of her Aunt by his attentions to her, without considering what effect they might have on the Lady herself. He would always sit by her when she was in the room, appear dissatisfied if she left it, and was the first to enquire whether she meant soon to return. He was delighted with her Drawings, and enchanted with her performance on the Harpsichord; Everything that she said, appeared to interest him; his Conversation was addressed to her alone, and she seemed to be the sole object of his attention. That such efforts should succeed with one so tremblingly alive to every alarm of the kind as Mrs Percival, is by no means unnatural, and that they should have equal influence with her Neice whose imagination was lively, and whose Disposition romantic, who was already extremely pleased with him, and of course desirous that he might be so with her, is as little to be wondered at. Every moment as it added to the conviction of his liking her, made him still more pleasing, and strengthened in her Mind a wish of knowing him better. As for Mrs Percival, she was in tortures the whole Day; Nothing that she had ever felt before on a similar occasion was to be compared to the sensations which then distracted her; her fears had never been so strongly, or indeed so reasonably excited.—Her dislike of Stanly, her anger at her Neice, her impatience to have them separated conquered every idea of propriety & Goodbreeding, and though he had never mentioned any intention of leaving them the next day, she could not help asking him after Dinner, in her eagerness to have him gone, at what time he meant to set out.

"Oh! Ma'am, replied he, if I am off by twelve at night, you may think yourself lucky; and if I am not, you can only blame yourself for having left so much as the *hour* of my departure to my own disposal." Mrs Percival coloured very highly at this speech, and without addressing herself to any one in particular, immediately began a long harangue on the shocking behaviour of modern young Men, & the wonderful Alteration that had taken place in them, since her time, which she illustrated with many instructive anecdotes of the Decorum & Modesty which had marked the Characters of those whom she had known, when she had been young. This however did not prevent his walking in the Garden with her Neice, without any other companion for nearly an hour in the course of the Evening. They had left the room for that purpose with Camilla at a time when Mrs Peterson had been out of it, nor was it for some time after her return to it, that she could discover where they were. Camilla had taken two or three turns with them in the walk which led to the Arbour, but soon growing tired of listening to a Conversation in which she was seldom invited to join, & from its turning occasionally on Books, very little able to do it, she left them together in the arbour, to wander alone to some other part of the Garden, to eat the fruit, & examine Mrs Peterson's Greenhouse. Her absence was so far from being regretted, that it was scarcely noticed by them, & they continued conversing together on almost every subject, for Stanley seldom dwelt long on any, and had something to say on all, till they were interrupted by her Aunt.

Kitty was by this time perfectly convinced that both in Natural Abilities, & acquired information, Edward Stanley was infinitely superior to his Sister. Her desire of knowing that he was so, had induced her to take every opportunity of turning the Conversation on History and they were very soon engaged in an historical dispute, for which no one was more calculated than Stanley who was so far from being really of any party, that he had scarcely a fixed opinion on the Subject. He could therefore always take either side, & always argue with temper. In his indifference on all such topics he was very unlike his Companion, whose judgement being guided by her feelings which were eager & warm, was easily decided, and though it was not always infallible, she defended it with a Spirit & Enthuisasm[25] which marked her own reliance on it. They had continued therefore for sometime conversing in this manner on the character of Richard the 3d, which he was warmly defending when he suddenly seized hold of her hand, and exclaiming with great emotion, "Upon my honour you are entirely mistaken," pressed it passionately to his lips, & ran out of the arbour. Astonished at this behaviour, for which she was wholly unable to account, she continued for a few Moments motionless on the seat where he had left her, and was then on the point of following him up the narrow walk through which he had passed, when on looking up the one that lay immediately before the arbour, she saw her Aunt walking towards her with more than her usual quickness. This explained at once the reason of his leaving her, but his leaving her in such Manner was rendered still more inexplicable by it. She felt a considerable degree of confusion at having been seen by her in such a place with Edward, and at having that part of his conduct, for which she could not herself account, witnessed by one to whom all gallantry was odious. She remained therefore confused and distressed & irresolute, and suffered her Aunt to approach her, without leaving the Arbour. Mrs Percival's looks were by no means calculated to animate the spirits of her Neice, who in silence awaited her accusation, and in silence meditated her Defence. After a few Moments suspence, for Mrs Peterson was too much fatigued to speak immediately, she began with great Anger and Asperity, the following harangue. "Well; *this* is beyond anything I could have supposed. *Profligate* as I *knew* you to be, I was not prepared for such a sight. This is beyond any thing you ever did *before;* beyond any thing I ever heard of in my Life! Such Impudence, I never witnessed before in such a Girl! And this is the reward for all the cares I have taken in your Education; for all my troubles & Anxieties; and Heaven knows how many they have been! All I wished for, was to breed you up virtuously; I never wanted you to play upon the Harpsichord, or draw better than any one else; but I had hoped to see you respectable and good; to see you able & willing to give an example of Modesty and Virtue to the Young people here abouts. I bought you Blair's Sermons, and Cœlebs in

25 *sic.*

Search of a Wife,[26] I gave you the key to my own Library, and borrowed a great many good books of my Neighbours for you, all to this purpose. But I might have spared myself the trouble—Oh! Catherine, you are an abandoned Creature, and I do not know what will become of you. I am glad however, she continued softening into some degree of Mildness, to see that you have some shame for what you have done, and if you are really sorry for it, and your future life is a life of penitence and reformation perhaps you may be forgiven. But I plainly see that every thing is going to sixes & sevens and all order will soon be at an end throughout the Kingdom."

"Not however Ma'am the sooner, I hope, from any conduct of mine, said Catherine in a tone of great humility, for upon my honour I have done nothing this evening that can contribute to overthrow the establishment of the kingdom."

"You are Mistaken Child, replied she; the welfare of every Nation depends upon the virtue of it's individuals, and any one who offends in so gross a manner against decorum & propriety is certainly hastening it's ruin. You have been giving a bad example to the World, and the World is but too well disposed to receive such."

"Pardon me Madam, said her Neice; but I *can* have given an Example only to *You,* for You alone have seen the offence. Upon my word however there is no danger to fear from what I have done; Mr Stanley's behaviour has given me as much surprise, as it has done to You, and I can only suppose that it was the effect of his high spirits, authorized in his opinion by our relationship. But do you consider Madam that it is growing very late? Indeed You had better return to the house." This speech as she well knew, would be unanswerable with her Aunt, who instantly rose, and hurried away under so many apprehensions for her own health, as banished for the time all anxiety about her Neice, who walked quietly by her side, revolving within her own Mind the occurrence that had given her Aunt so much alarm. "I am astonished at my own imprudence, said Mrs Percival; How could I be so forgetful as to sit down out of doors at such a time of night. I shall certainly have a return of my rheumatism after it—I begin to feel very chill already. I must have caught a dreadful cold by this time—I am sure of being lain-up all the winter after it—" Then reckoning with her fingers, "Let me see; This is July; the cold weather will soon be coming in—August—September—October—November—December—January—February—March—April—Very likely I may not be tolerable again before May. I must and will have that arbour pulled down—it will be the death of me; who knows *now,* but what I may never recover—Such things *have* happened—My particular freind Miss Sarah Hutchinson's death was occasioned by nothing more—She staid out late one Evening in April, and got wet through for it rained very hard, and never changed her Cloathes when she came home—It is unknown how many people have died in consequence of catching Cold! I do not beleive there is a disorder in the World except the Smallpox which does not spring from it." It was in vain that Kitty endeavoured to convince her

26 Cœlebs *etc. substituted for* Seccar's explanation of the Catechism.

that her fears on the occasion were groundless; that it was not yet late enough to catch cold, and that even if it were, she might hope to escape any other complaint, and to recover in less than ten Months. Mrs Percival only replied that she hoped she knew more of Ill health than to be convinced in such a point by a Girl who had always been perfectly well, and hurried up stairs leaving Kitty to make her apologies to Mr & Mrs Stanley for going to bed—. Tho' Mrs Percival seemed perfectly satisfied with the goodness of the Apology herself, yet Kitty felt somewhat embarrassed to find that the only one she could offer to their Visitors was that her Aunt had *perhaps* caught cold, for Mrs Peterson charged her to make light of it, for fear of alarming them. Mr & Mrs Stanley however who well knew that their Cousin was easily terrified on that Score, received the account of it with very little surprise, and all proper concern. Edward & his Sister soon came in, & Kitty had no difficulty in gaining an explanation of his Conduct from him, for he was too warm on the subject himself, and too eager to learn its success, to refrain from making immediate Enquiries about it; & She could not help feeling both surprised & offended at the ease & Indifference with which he owned that all his intentions had been to frighten her Aunt by pretending an affection for *her*, a design so very incompatible with that partiality which she had at one time been almost convinced of his feeling for her. It is true that she had not yet seen enough of him to be actually in love with him, yet she felt greatly disappointed that so handsome, so elegant, so lively a young Man should be so perfectly free from any such Sentiment as to make it his principal Sport. There was a Novelty in his character which to *her* was extremely pleasing; his person was uncommonly fine, his Spirits & Vivacity suited to her own, and his Manners at once so animated & insinuating, that she thought it must be impossible for him to be otherwise than amiable, and was ready to give him Credit for being perfectly so. He knew the powers of them himself; to them he had often been endebted for his father's forgiveness of faults which had he been awkward & inelegant would have appeared very serious; to them, even more than to his person or his fortune, he owed the regard which almost every one was disposed to feel for him, and which Young Women in particular were inclined to entertain. Their influence was acknowledged on the present occasion by Kitty, whose Anger they entirely dispelled, and whose Chearfulness they had power not only to restore, but to raise—. The Evening passed off as agreably as the one that had preceded it; they continued talking to each other, during the cheif part of it, and such was the power of his Address, & the Brilliancy of his Eyes, that when they parted for the Night, tho' Catherine had but a few hours before totally given up the idea, yet she felt almost convinced again that he was really in love with her. She reflected on their past Conversation, and tho' it had been on various & indifferent subjects, and she could not exactly recollect any speech on his side expressive of such a partiality, she was still however nearly certain of it's being so; But fearful of being vain enough to suppose such a thing without sufficient reason, she resolved to suspend her final determination on it, till the next day, and more especially till their parting which she thought would infallibly explain his regard if any he had—. The more she had seen of him, the more inclined was she to like him, & the more desirous that he should like *her.* She was convinced of his being naturally very clever and very well disposed, and that his thoughtlessness & negligence, which tho' they appeared to *her* as very becoming in *him,* she was aware would by many people be considered as defects in his Character, merely proceeded from a vivacity always pleasing in Young Men, & were far from testifying a weak or vacant Understanding. Having settled this point within herself, and being perfectly convinced by her own arguments of it's truth, she went to bed in high Spirits, determined to study his Character, and watch his Behaviour still more the next day. She got up with the same good resolutions and would probably have put them in execution, had not Anne informed her as soon as she entered the room that Mr Edward Stanley was already gone. At first she refused to credit the information, but when her Maid assured her that he had ordered a Carriage the evening before to be there at seven o'clock in the Morning and that she herself had actually seen him depart in it a little after eight, she could no longer deny her beleif to it. "And this, thought she to herself blushing with anger at her own folly, this is the affection for me of which I was so certain. Oh! what a silly Thing is Woman! How vain, how unreasonable! To suppose that a young Man would be seriously attached in the course of four & twenty hours, to a Girl who has nothing to recommend her but a good pair of eyes! And he is really gone! Gone perhaps without bestowing a thought on me! Oh! why was not I up by eight o'clock? But it is a proper punishment for my Lazyness & Folly, and I am heartily glad of it. I deserve it all, & ten times more for such insufferable vanity. It will at least be of service to me in that respect; it will teach me in future *not* to think Every Body is in love with me. Yet I *should* like to have seen him before he went, for perhaps it may be many Years before we meet again. By his Manner of leaving us however, he seems to have been perfectly indifferent about it. How very odd, that he should go without giving us Notice of it, or taking leave of any one! But it is just like a Young Man, governed by the whim of the moment, or actuated merely by the love of doing anything oddly! Unaccountable Beings indeed! And Young Women are equally ridiculous! I shall soon begin to think like my Aunt that everything is going to sixes & sevens, and that the whole race of Mankind are degenerating." She was just dressed, and on the point of leaving her room to make her personal enquiries after Mrs Peterson, when Miss Stanley knocked at her door, & on her being admitted began in her Usual Strain a long harangue upon her Father's being so shocking as to make Edward go at all, and upon Edward's being so horrid as to leave them at such an hour in the Morning. "You have no idea, said she, how surprised I was, when he came into my Room to bid me good bye—"

"Have you seen him then, this Morning?" said Kitty.

"Oh Yes! And I was so sleepy that I could not open my eyes. And so he said, Camilla, goodbye to you for I am going away—. I have not time to take leave of any body else, and I dare not trust myself to see Kitty, for then you know I should never get away—"

"Nonsense, said Kitty; he did not say that, or he was in joke if he did."

"Oh! no I assure you he was as much in earnest as he ever was in his life; he was too much out of spirits to joke *then.* And he desired me when we all met at Breakfast to give his Compts to your Aunt, and his Love to you, for you was a nice Girl he said, and he only wished it were in his power to be more with You. You were just the Girl to suit him, because you were so lively and good-natured, and he wished with all his heart that you might not be married before he came back, for there was nothing he liked better than being here. Oh! you have no idea what fine things he said about you, till at last I fell asleep and he went away. But he certainly is in love with you—I am sure he is—I have thought so a great while I assure You."

"How can you be so ridiculous? said Kitty smiling with pleasure; I do not beleive him to be so easily affected. But he *did* desire his Love to me then? And wished I might not be married before his return? And said I was a Nice Girl, did he?"

"Oh! dear, Yes, and I assure You it is the greatest praise in his opinion, that he can bestow on any body; I can hardly ever persuade him to call *me* one, tho' I beg him sometimes for an hour together."

"And do You really think that he was sorry to go?"

"Oh! you can have no idea how wretched it made him. He would not have gone this Month, if my Father had not insisted on it; Edward told me so himself yesterday. He said that he wished with all his heart he had never promised to go abroad, for that he repented it more and more every day; that it interfered with all his other schemes, and that since Papa had spoken to him about it, he was more unwilling to leave Chetwynde than ever."

"Did he really say all this? And why would your father insist upon his going? "His leaving England interfered with all his other plans, and his Conversation with Mr Stanley had made him still more averse to it." What can this Mean?" "Why that he is excessively in love with you to be sure; what other plans can he have? And I suppose my father said that if he had not been going abroad, he should have wished him to marry you immediately.—But I must go and see your Aunt's plants—There is one of them that I quite doat on—and two or three more besides—"

"Can Camilla's explanation be true? said Catherine to herself, when her freind had left the room. And after all my doubts and Uncertainties, can Stanley really be averse to leaving England for *my sake* only? "His plans interrupted." And what indeed can his plans be, but towards Marriage? Yet *so soon* to be in love with me!—But it is the effect perhaps only of a warmth of heart which to *me* is the highest recommendation in any one. A Heart disposed to love—And such under the appearance of so much Gaity and Inattention, is Stanly's! Oh! how much does it endear him to me! But he is gone—Gone perhaps for Years—Obliged to tear himself from what he most loves, his happiness is sacrificed to the vanity of his Father! In what anguish he must have left the house! Unable to see me, or to bid me adieu, while I, senseless wretch, was daring to sleep. This, then explained his leaving us at such a time of day—. He could not trust himself to see me—. Charming Young Man! How much must you have suffered! I *knew* that it was impossible for one so elegant, and so well bred, to leave any Family in such a Manner, but for a Motive like this unanswerable." Satisfied, beyond the power of Change, of this, She went in high spirits to her Aunt's apartment, without giving a Moment's recollection on the vanity of Young Women, or the unaccountable conduct of Young Men.

Kitty continued in this state of satisfaction during the remainder of the Stanley's visit—Who took their leave with many pressing invitations to visit them in London, when as Camilla said, she might have an opportunity of becoming acquainted with that sweet girl Augusta Hallifax—Or Rather (thought Kitty,) of seeing my dr Mary Wynn again—Mrs Percival in answer to Mrs Stanley's invitation replied—That she looked upon London as the hot house of Vice where virtue had long been banished from Society & wickedness of every description was daily gaining ground—that Kitty was of herself sufficiently inclined to give way to, & indulge in vicious inclinations—& therefore was the last girl in the world to be trusted in London, as she would be totally unable to withstand temptation——

After the departure of the Stanleys Kitty returned to her usual occupations, but Alas! they had lost their power of pleasing. Her bower alone retained its interest in her feelings, & perhaps that was oweing to the particular remembrance it brought to her mind of Edwd Stanley.

The Summer passed away unmarked by any incident worth narrating, or any pleasure to Catharine save one, which arose from the reciept of a letter from her friend Cecilia now Mrs Lascelles, announcing the speedy return of herself & Husband to England.

A correspondance productive indeed of little pleasure to either party had been established between Camilla & Catharine. The latter had now lost the only satisfaction she had ever received from the letters of Miss Stanley, as that young Lady having informed her Friend of the departure of her Brother to Lyons now never mentioned his name—Her letters seldom contained any Intelligence except a description of some new Article of Dress, an enumeration of various engagements, a panegyric (?) on Augusta Halifax & perhaps a little abuse of the unfortunate Sir Peter—

The Grove, for so was the Mansion of Mrs Percival at Chetwynde denominated was situated whin five miles from Exeter, but though that Lady possessed a carriage & horses of her [her] own, it was seldom that Catharine could prevail on her to visit that town for the purpose of shopping, on account of the many Officers perpetually Quartered there & infested the principal Streets—A company of strolling players in their way from some Neighbouring Races having opened a temporary Theatre there, Mrs Percival was prevailed on by her Niece to indulge her by attending the performance once during their stay—Mrs Percival insisted on paying Miss Dudley the compliment of inviting her to join the party, when a new difficulty arose, from the necessity of having some Gentleman to attend them——

*Here follows a contribution to Evelyn by Jane Austen's niece Anna Lefroy.*

On re entering his circular domain, his round-Robin of perpetual peace; where enjoyment had no end, and calamity no commencement, his spirits became wonderfully composed, and a delicious calm extended itself through every nerve—With his pocket hankerchief (once hemmed by the genius of the too susceptible Rosa) he wiped the morbid moisture from his brow;—then flew to the Boudoir of his Maria—And, did *she* not fly to meet her Frederick? Did she not dart from the Couch on which she had so gracefully reclined, and, bounding like an agile Fawn over the intervening Foot stool, precipitate herself into his arms? Does she not, though fainting between every syllable, breathe forth as it were by installments her Frederick's adored name? Who is there of perception so obtuse as not to realize the touching scene? Who, of ear so dull as not to catch the soft murmur of Maria's voice? Ah! Who? The heart of every sympathetic reader repeats, Ah, Who? Vain Echo! Vain sympathy! There is no Meeting—no Murmur—No Maria—It is not in the power of language however potent; nor in that of style, however diffuse to render justice to the astonishment of Mr Gower—Arming himself with a mahogany ruler which some fatality had placed on Maria's writing table, and calling repeatedly on her beloved Name, he rushed forward to examine the adjacent apartments—In the Dressing room of his lost one he had the melancholy satisfaction of picking up a curl paper, and a gust of wind, as he re entered the Boudoir, swept from the table, & placed at his feet a skein of black sewing silk—These were the only traces of Maria!! Carefully locking the doors of these now desolate rooms, burying the key deep in his Waistcoat pocket, & the mystery of Maria's disappearance yet deeper in his heart of hearts, Mr Gower left his once happy home, and sought a supper, and a Bed, at the house of the hospitable Mrs Willis—There was an oppression on his chest which made him extremely uncomfortable; he regretted that instead of the skein of silk carefully wrapped up in the curl paper & placed beneath his pillow he had not rather swallowed Laudanum—It would have been, in all probability, more efficacious—At last, Mr Gower slept a troubled sleep, and in due course of time he dreamt a troubled dream—He dreamed of Maria, as how could he less? She stood by his Bed side, in her Dressing Gown—one hand held an open book, with the forefinger of the other she pointed to this ominous passage—"Tantôt c'est un vide; qui nous ennuie; tantôt c'est un poids qui nous oppresse"—The unfortunate Frederick uttered a deep groan—& as the vision closed the volume he observed these characters strangely imprinted on the Cover—Rolandi—Berners Street. *Who* was this dangerous Rolandi? Doubtless a Bravo or a Monk—possibly both—and what was he to Maria? Vainly he would have dared the worst, and put the fatal question—the semblance of Maria raised her monitory finger, and interdicted speech—Yet, some words she spoke, or seemed to speak her self; Mr Gower could distinguish only these—Search—Cupboard—Top shelf—Once more he essayed to speak, but it was all bewilderment—He heard strange Demon-like Sounds; hissing and spitting—he smelt an unearthly smell the agony became unbearable, and he awoke—Maria had vanished; the Rush light was expiring in the Socket; and the benevolent Mrs Willis entering his room, threw open the shutters, and in accordance with her own warmth of heart admitted the full blaze of a Summer morning's Sun—But what found he on reentering that circle of peace, that round Robin of perpetual peace

J. A. E. L.